COLOSSIANS
EXPLAINED

Kakra Baiden

Simple. Practical. Anointed.

Copyright © 2025 by Kakra Baiden

Colossians Explained
by Kakra Baiden

Printed in the United States of America

ISBN 978-1-945123-29-0

All rights reserved. No part of this document may be reproduced or transmitted in any form, by any means (electronic, photocopying, recording, or otherwise) without the written permission of the author.

Unless otherwise indicated, Bible quotations are taken from the King James Version of the Bible. Public domain.

DEDICATION

This book is dedicated to my brothers: Jude Baiden, Moses Baiden, and my twin brother, Panyin Baiden. I love you all.

TABLE OF CONTENTS

Introduction vii
Colossians Chapter 1.. 1
Colossians Chapter 2.. 47
Colossians Chapter 3.. 77
Colossians Chapter 4.. 117
Conclusion 139

INTRODUCTION

To help us understand the book of Colossians and get the most out of it, let's briefly walk through how we're going to study it.

1. By Context

This refers to the information, circumstances, and events surrounding each verse. This is important because you can form your own opinion and collect unrelated and out-of-context verses to support them. This will lead to a distortion of God's Word.

We will use the following contexts:

a. The verse itself.
b. The chapter the verse is found in.
c. The book, in this case, the book of Colossians.
d. All the 66 books of the Bible, because they represent the whole counsel of God.

2. The Holy Spirit

We will be relying on the Holy Spirit to teach us. He is the Master Teacher who can produce the intended results. Jesus said, "He will guide you into all truth" (John 16:13).

3. Subtitles and Points

I will be using subtitles and points to arrange the logical structure and also to break it down into smaller bits so it can be "spiritually digestible."

4. Practical Application

The Bible is set in human experience because God wanted it to be applicable to us. I will be making practical applications and sharing stories and testimonies. I will also be praying concerning different aspects of life, and I pray you experience miracles, signs, and wonders.

5. Background to the Book of Colossians

Paul wrote this letter from prison to the church in Colossae, a city in Asia Minor, present-day Turkey. He did not establish this church himself; it was established by Epaphras, a fellow laborer of Paul. He wrote this letter to establish them in their newfound faith.

LET'S PRAY BEFORE YOU BEGIN

Heavenly Father, I pray that the Holy Spirit will teach everyone who takes time to go through this book. Grant them revelation and insight into Your Word, and may their lives never be the same again. Let them experience healing, miracles, signs, and wonders as they read, in Jesus' name. Amen.

COLOSSIANS CHAPTER 1

Colossians 1:1

"Paul, an apostle of Jesus Christ by the will of God, and Timotheus our brother."

WHO IS AN APOSTLE?

"Paul, an apostle"
An apostle is a messenger, a representative of the Lord or the church, sent to accomplish a specific mission.

1. Jesus Is an Apostle

Jesus Himself is called an apostle. "Consider the Apostle and High Priest of our profession, Christ Jesus, Who was faithful to him that appointed him" (Hebrews 3:1-2). Jesus was sent by God from heaven to earth to fulfill a mission: to save sinners. "Christ Jesus came into the world to save sinners; of whom I am chief" (1 Timothy 1:15).

In modern times, when we hear "apostle," we might think of someone who plants churches. But in biblical terms, it means a messenger.

2. Epaphroditus Was an Apostle

He was a member of the church of Philippi. Paul described him as "my brother, and companion in labour, and fellowsoldier, but your messenger" (Philippians 2:25). The Greek word *apostello* used here signifies that he was sent, not to preach, but to assist Paul in ministry. Epaphroditus acted more like a deacon, responsible for the practical work of the church.

Even if you're serving in a simple role, like an usher or a cleaner, remember: You are sent by God, and your service carries the title "apostle." Your work is significant, and there is a great reward awaiting you. Understanding this keeps you from feeling unappreciated and reminds you of the importance of your role in God's Kingdom.

YOU DON'T CHOOSE YOUR MINISTRY

"By the will of God"
Paul didn't choose to be an apostle—God chose him. Similarly, in my own experience, I never prayed or desired to be a minister.

I Saw Jesus
One night, while praying on the rooftop around 3:00 a.m., the heavens suddenly opened. The darkness turned to light, like Paul's encounter, "At midday, O king, I saw in the way a light from heaven, above the brightness of the sun" (Acts 26:13).

Jesus appeared to me and said, "I have called you to be a minister of God." It wasn't my intention. My family was full of businessmen, and my goal was to study architecture and later go into business. But God had other plans. From that day on, I followed His will, not mine.

"And God hath set some in the church, first apostles, secondarily prophets, thirdly teachers" (1 Corinthians 12:28) and so on. God "set" us—He placed us. Just as each body part is created for a specific function (ears don't choose to be ears; they are made as ears), so it is with us in the body of Christ.

Don't be frustrated trying to become something God hasn't called you to be. Instead, seek God's will and purpose for your life. When we do that, we enjoy His grace. Just as my ear doesn't struggle to hear, we don't have to struggle in our God-given roles. Paul understood that he was chosen by God, and so must we understand that our service in the Kingdom is appointed by Him.

PAUL INTRODUCES TIMOTHY

"Timotheus our brother"
Timothy was with Paul, serving as his travel companion and amanuensis, which is like a secretary. Picture this: Paul is pacing around the room, speaking, and Timothy is writing everything down. In fact, most of Paul's letters were dictated to Timothy, who faithfully transcribed them.

Paul calls him "our brother." Here, "brother" doesn't mean a biological sibling but rather a spiritual brother. Have you noticed that even if you are travelling across the world, there is a special connection when you meet another Christian? It's because we share the same heavenly Father. "The Spirit itself beareth witness with our spirit, that we are the children of God" (Romans 8:16).

No matter where I travel—different countries, different nationalities—when I meet a fellow believer, the Holy Spirit confirms to me that this person is my brother or sister. We are part of the same spiritual family.

Colossians 1:2
"To the saints and faithful brethren in Christ which are at Colosse: Grace be unto you, and peace, from God our Father and the Lord Jesus Christ."

WHO THE LETTER IS WRITTEN TO

1. "To the Saints"

The word "saint" means a holy person and not a dead person who once lived a holy life. It is applied to living Christians. It comes from the root word "sanctify," which means to make holy. Jesus is described as the One who "washed us from our sins in his own blood" (Revelation 1:5). Becoming a saint starts with being born again. "If thou shalt confess with thy mouth the Lord Jesus, and shalt believe in thine heart that God hath raised him from the dead, thou shalt be saved. For with the heart man believeth unto righteousness; and with the mouth confession is made unto salvation" (Romans 10:9-10).

My Salvation Experience
I still remember the day I became born again over 30 years ago. My pastor, Dag Heward-Mills, visited our house to see my sister, who was then his friend. As he spoke to me about Jesus, he asked, "Are you born again?" When I said no, he shared how Christ died for my sins. After talking for a while, he asked if I wanted to be born again, and I said yes. That day, I believed in Jesus with my heart and confessed Him with my mouth, and I became born again.

"Except a man be born again, he cannot see the kingdom of God" (John 3:3). Being born again is not the same as merely attending church or giving offerings. It means repenting of your sins and being washed by the blood. It is having a personal relationship with Jesus as your Lord and Savior.

2. Faithful Brethren in Christ

"Faithful" means trustworthy. Every relationship is built on trust. Imagine you're in a serious relationship, and one day you find a suspicious message on your partner's phone. Even if you love them, your trust will be shaken because trust is foundational. When trust is broken, a person may be physically present, but their heart is gone.

Paul emphasizes that the letter is written to saints who are also faithful—faithful to the Lord. Jesus' rewards are based on faithfulness: "Well done, good and faithful servant" (Matthew 25:21). The word "good" refers to being holy, and "faithful" means dependable. God expects us to be trustworthy, or faithful to Him. Are you faithful to Jesus?

You can easily find people who are skilled in various fields—sports, technology, finance, but finding a truly faithful person is rare. It is difficult to find a faithful spouse, a faithful friend, or a faithful worker. "Most men will proclaim every one his own goodness: but a faithful man who can find?" (Proverbs 20:6).

Let's be committed to God in our actions and thoughts. Let's serve Him sincerely, knowing that one day we'll hear, "Well done, good and faithful servant." Even in secret, let's be honest and upright, because all secrets will eventually be revealed.

TWO IMPORTANT PRAYERS

1. Prayer for Grace

"Grace be unto you"

Paul offers two prayers for the Colossians, and the first is for grace. The more I grow, the more I realize how much we need grace. Without God's help, we can accomplish very little on our own. Human beings control very little in life; we cannot even guarantee that we'll be alive in the next five minutes.

Life is fragile and fleeting. "For all flesh is as grass, and all the glory of man as the flower of grass. The grass withereth, and the flower thereof falleth away" (1 Peter 1:24). This verse reminds us that we are weak and fragile—like grass that can disappear overnight. That's why we need God's grace.

Whether you're getting married, writing an exam, or raising children, you need God's help.

My Friend Who Missed the Exams

I remember a friend who didn't know the Lord while studying architecture at the university. Before an important exam, I suggested we go and pray together, but he said, "Pastor, I want to sleep for 30 more minutes." So, I went to pray, took a shower, and then went to write the exam.

When I returned, he was still asleep. He had missed the exam, and because of that, he had to wait an entire year to retake that particular exam. Grace eluded him in that moment. We need God's grace for everything. May God's grace cover you in your family, finances, and life.

The Best Definition of Grace

There are many definitions of grace, but the best definition of grace can be found in Ephesians 2:8-9: "For by grace are ye saved through faith; and that not of yourselves: it is the gift of God: not of works, lest any man should boast." In other words, grace produces results not based on our own efforts.

The Bible says, "For we are his workmanship, created in Christ Jesus unto good works, which God hath before ordained that we should walk in them" (Ephesians 2:10). A workmanship is something crafted by someone else. When you're under God's grace, He produces results in your life that you could not accomplish alone.

2. Prayer for Peace

"And peace"

The second prayer Paul prays for them is for peace. Peace is essential. Without peace, you can't enjoy anything—not even the simplest pleasures. If your mind is troubled, you can't even focus on a movie or enjoy your food. The Bible says, "For the kingdom of God is not meat and drink; but righteousness, and peace, and joy in the Holy Ghost" (Romans 14:17). Even with meat and drink, you need peace and joy to enjoy them. Paul prays for peace because he understands how valuable it is.

Do you know that the world spends billions of dollars every year in pursuit of peace? But true peace only comes from God. "I will both lay me down in peace, and sleep: for thou, LORD, only makest me dwell in safety" (Psalm 4:8).

The Difference Between the Peace of God and the Peace of the World

Worldly peace depends on circumstances, while God's peace depends on His presence. The Bible refers to Jesus as the "Prince of Peace" (Isaiah 9:6), meaning He rules over peace. He's the source of peace, not a situation or condition. "Peace I leave with you, my peace I give unto you: not as the world giveth, give I unto you. Let not your heart be troubled, neither let it be afraid" (John 14:27). Jesus doesn't give us circumstantial peace; He gives us His presence. You can be in the middle of a crisis and still have peace because God is with you.

When a storm arose as Jesus and His disciples were on a boat, Jesus was asleep, completely at peace. The disciples woke Him in panic, but He rebuked the storm and brought calm. His peace wasn't based on circumstances; it was rooted in the presence of God. May your peace also come from the Holy Spirit.

My Experience of God's Peace

I remember flying to America years ago. While crossing the Atlantic, the plane developed an engine problem. The passengers were anxious, but I felt a strange peace. I told the woman sitting beside me, "We will not die; God will save us." She started sharing my words with others, and soon a crowd gathered around me for comfort. While others were anxious, I was at peace, knowing God was with us. Their peace depended on circumstances; mine was based on God's presence.

Let's pursue the peace of God; it's not a circumstance, but a person. His name is Jesus. Like David, we can say, "I will both lay me down in peace, and sleep: for thou, LORD, only makest me dwell in safety" (Psalm 4:8).

Colossians 1:3
"We give thanks to God and the Father of our Lord Jesus Christ, praying always for you."

THE IMPORTANCE OF THANKSGIVING

1. We Must Thank God for Being a Father

"We give thanks to God and the Father"

Jesus was the first to introduce God as a father. In the Old Testament, God revealed Himself as "I Am" and "Jehovah." But Jesus consistently called God "Father," revealing His role in our lives. We have to thank God for His fatherly role.

In the Lord's prayer, Jesus teaches us to pray, "Our Father which art in heaven, Hallowed be thy name. Thy kingdom come, Thy will be done in earth, as it is in heaven. Give us this day our daily bread. And forgive us our debts, as we forgive our debtors. And lead us not into temptation, but deliver us from evil" (Matthew 6:9-13). In this short prayer, Jesus reveals God's role as our Father. Let's look at it in detail.

a. Provision: *"Give us this day our daily bread."*

Life itself is God's provision. Before we even consider food, houses, or wealth, let's appreciate the gift of life. One day, the Holy Spirit said to me, "Do you know why you wake up every morning?" I asked, "Why?" He replied, "I wake you up every morning. Otherwise, you would die in your sleep. "He wakeneth morning by morning, he wakeneth mine ear to hear as the learned" (Isaiah 50:4). God not only wakes us up, but He also speaks to us. We are alive today because God gave us life, which is the most precious gift of all.

b. Guidance: *"Lead us not into temptation."*

One of the main roles of a father is guidance. "My son, hear the instruction of thy father, and forsake not the law of thy mother: For they shall be an ornament of grace unto thy head, and chains about thy neck" (Proverbs 1:8-9).

Guidance makes things easy for children; grace. Guidance makes you blessed; chains about your neck.

I thank God for a good biological father who guided me to become who I am today.

We must allow God to guide us through His Word and His Spirit.

c. Protection: *"Deliver us from evil."*

Our heavenly Father protects us with His wisdom and power. When I was young, my dad forbade me from making certain friends because he was protecting me from evil. Today, when I look back, I am grateful.

Take a moment to thank God for His fatherly care. Lift your hands and give thanks. Father, we thank You for being our Father. We bless You for all that You do. For life, provision, guidance, and protection. Thank You for the blessings we often take for granted. We thank You in Jesus' mighty name. Amen.

2. We Must Thank the Lord Jesus Christ

"To our Lord Jesus Christ"

The term "Lord" signifies someone who has authority over you. I remember speaking to a young man in my church who expressed immense gratitude after I gave him advice. He explained that he didn't have anyone to guide him. At just 14 years old, he was living on his own because his parents were absent. He told me, "I don't even know what is right and what is wrong, but your direction means so much to me because I have no authority figure in my life."

That conversation struck me. Think about children who grow up without responsible parents. They are more likely to become wayward because there is no one guiding them. Jesus, as our Lord, has authority over us, and His authority is for our benefit. "If thou shalt confess with thy mouth the Lord Jesus, and shalt believe in thine heart that God hath raised him from the dead, thou shalt be saved" (Romans 10:9). His lordship brings blessings, not destruction.

Example of the Prodigal Son

Consider the story of the prodigal son. One son chose to live outside his father's authority. He took his inheritance, left home, and squandered all his money, becoming destitute. Why did this happen? Because he chose to live outside the protective authority of his father. When we submit to God's authority, it's for our own good. Imagine a child who rebels against their parents' authority—it's unlikely that the child will thrive. Similarly, God's authority keeps us on the right path.

Paul said we should thank Jesus for His lordship. Just think: If Jesus hadn't taken control of our lives early on, some of us might have made many regretful choices. For instance, you might have had kids when you were in your teens and not ready.

Colossians 1:4

"Since we heard of your faith in Christ Jesus, and of the love which ye have to all the saints."

REASONS FOR THANKSGIVING

1. Faith (Salvation)

"We heard of your faith in Christ Jesus"

These are powerful thanksgiving points you can use in your personal prayer. Paul first mentions that he has heard about their faith. They had been born again, and this news filled him with joy.

I remember when one of my friends, who wasn't a believer, came to my room to announce that he had become born again. Another friend later came to share the same news. I was overjoyed because these were my friends who had once rejected Christ. Hearing that they had given their lives to Jesus was an immense source of happiness. Don't forget to thank God for anyone you know who is saved.

The Assassins Who Got Converted

One time, I was preaching somewhere, and some assassins had followed a target into the church. They intended to kill this person. However, as they listened to the sermon, their hearts were changed. By the end of the message, they came forward, confessed their sins, gave their lives to Christ, and decided not to commit the murder. What a miracle!

I witnessed this transformation with my own eyes. When we hear stories of such dramatic conversions, we can't help but give thanks to God. Paul felt the same way when he heard about the Colossians' faith.

2. Love

"The love which ye have to all the saints"

Paul also commended the Colossians for their love for others. One of the greatest proofs of our love for God is how we treat other people. "If a man say, I love God, and hateth his brother, he is a liar: for he that loveth not his brother whom he hath seen, how can he love God whom he hath not seen?" (1 John 4:20). True love for God manifests in our love for other people.

For example, a nasty husband who becomes born again often changes and starts to show genuine love to his wife and children. Rebellious children who come to Christ become more loving and respectful toward their parents. Love for others is a sign that someone has experienced true spiritual transformation. Let's thank God for the love of parents, spouses, children, and friends.

A lawyer asked Jesus, "Master, which is the great commandment in the law?" Jesus replied, "Thou shalt love the Lord thy God with all thy heart, and with all thy soul, and with all thy mind… And the second is like unto it, Thou shalt love thy neighbour as thyself" (Matthew 22:35-39). Loving God naturally leads to loving His children. Paul was thrilled to hear that the Colossians displayed this kind of love.

Colossians 1:5

"For the hope which is laid up for you in heaven, whereof ye heard before in the word of the truth of the gospel."

THE HOPE OF CHRISTIANS

1. Being a Believer Isn't a Hopeless Endeavor

"For the hope which is laid up for you in heaven"

There is a great reward awaiting us. Our hope is securely laid up in heaven. It's not subject to decay or theft, unlike earthly treasures. Jesus said, "Lay not up for yourselves treasures upon earth, where moth and rust doth corrupt, and where thieves break through and steal: But lay up for yourselves treasures in heaven, where neither moth nor rust doth corrupt, and where thieves do not break through nor steal" (Matthew 6:19-20).

I'm thankful that our eternal treasures are secure. Just as we put our money in a bank to keep it safe, God has secured our reward in heaven. No economic crisis or war can destroy it.

I Went to Heaven

One day I had a vision where I saw myself in heaven. I saw beautiful mansions and I remember entering the mansion of one of our Sunday school teachers, Jackie. The angel escorting me said, "Your house is completed when you die."

In the book of Revelation John said, "And I heard a voice from heaven saying unto me, Write, Blessed are the dead which die in the Lord from henceforth: Yea, saith the Spirit, that they may rest from their labours; and their works do follow them" (Revelation 14:13). It was a wonderful experience.

2. Our Hope Is Rooted in the Word of God

"In the word of the truth of the gospel"

Scripture or truth gives us a glimpse of what awaits us as believers. Take the story of Lazarus and the rich man in Luke 16:19-24. It teaches us about life after death and the hope of heaven. While Lazarus was comforted, the rich man found himself in torment. This story reminds us of the eternal hope we have in Christ.

My Vision of Heaven

By the grace of God, I've had visions of heaven. Once, I saw a beautiful mountain, which I believe is Mount Zion. "But ye are come unto mount Sion, and unto the city of the living God, the heavenly Jerusalem" (Hebrews 12:22). The grass was vibrant and resilient, springing back to its original form after being stepped on. I also saw magnificent mansions, just as Jesus promised. "In my Father's house are many mansions" (John 14:2).

Heaven is a glorious place, free from sickness, pain, and death. "And God shall wipe away all tears from their eyes; and there shall be no more death, neither sorrow, nor crying, neither shall there be any more pain: for the former things are passed away" (Revelation 21:4).

Paul wanted the Colossians to know that their faith was not in vain. We, too, should hold on to our faith, knowing that heaven awaits us.

Colossians 1:6

"Which is come unto you, as it is in all the world; and bringeth forth fruit, as it doth also in you, since the day ye heard of it, and knew the grace of God in truth."

GOD'S WORD PRODUCES THE FOLLOWING

1. Fruit

"Bringeth forth fruit"

Hope in God produces the fruit of the Spirit. "But the fruit of the Spirit is love, joy, peace, longsuffering, gentleness, goodness, faith, Meekness, temperance: against such there is no law" (Galatians 5:22-23). As a married man, I strive to exhibit these qualities in my home, because I want to be ready to meet Jesus and hear Him say, "Well done." Knowing there is judgment after death motivates me to live a godly life and forgive others.

2. Grace

"Knew the grace of God in truth"

Salvation and the truth of God's Word produce grace and enable us to bear fruit. Salvation breaks the power of sin, and grace empowers us to live for God. What a wonderful promise! Grace helps us become the people God wants us to be.

I pray that you will embrace this hope, let it transform your life, and hold onto the promises of God.

Colossians 1:7
"As ye also learned of Epaphras our dear fellowservant, who is for you a faithful minister of Christ."

PAUL'S TESTIMONY ABOUT EPAPHRAS

1. He Was a "Fellowservant"

The Greek word used here is *syndoulos*, which means "a fellow slave." The root "syn" relates to the English word "sync," indicating a connection or being in harmony with someone else. Paul was saying that both he and Epaphras were slaves to the same Master—Jesus Christ.

A slave has no will of their own. Jesus exemplified this where He said, "Not my will, but thine, be done" (Luke 22:42). To be a good Christian, like Epaphras, we must submit our will entirely to God. This means that God's Word dictates our choices: whom we befriend, how we react when we're angry, the clothes we wear, and even our life decisions. We must allow God to guide us.

If you're looking for a spouse, a career, or direction in life, may the Lord be the One to guide you—because His choices are always best.

2. He Was a "Faithful Minister"

The word "minister" in Greek is *diakonos*, or "deacon." It literally means to run an errand, someone responsible for the physical work of the church. Deacons took care of physical matters of the church, while elders or pastors focused on spiritual duties.

When there was contention among the church about serving of tables, this was the response of the apostle: "It is not reason that we should leave the word of God, and serve tables. Wherefore, brethren, look ye out among you seven men of honest report, full of the Holy Ghost and wisdom, whom we may appoint over this business. But we will give ourselves continually to prayer, and to the ministry of the word" (Acts 6:2-4). Deacons, like Stephen, were chosen to handle physical tasks so that the apostles could focus on the spiritual work.

This reminds me of Epaphraditous a member of the Philippian church who was sent to care for Paul. He cooked for him, washed his clothes, and ensured he was taken care of. He combined the roles of a pastor and a deacon, much like Judas Iscariot did. Judas managed the money and helped with practical needs while also being an apostle.

If you're involved in practical work for your church—buying construction materials, setting up chairs, or managing logistics—you are fulfilling the role of a deacon. Remember, the Levites in Moses' time did similar work. There were only five priests, including Aaron and his sons, while the rest were Levites tasked with practical duties like carrying the tabernacle and washing the blood from the sacrifices that were been made.

These roles are essential and are just as significant as preaching. If you are a pastor of a church, you must understand that people who assist with parking cars or setting up equipment are equally doing God's work.

Colossians 1:8
"Who also declared unto us your love in the Spirit."

THE IMPORTANCE OF A GOOD TESTIMONY

Epaphras testified about the love of the Colossians. This love wasn't a fleeting, emotional affection, but a spiritual love, rooted in the fruit of the Spirit. True biblical love is not based on feelings but on a decision of the will. It is a commandment. "He that loveth not his brother whom he hath seen, how can he love God whom he hath not seen?" (1 John 4:20).

Love is an act of the will. You choose to love even when you don't feel like it, because it pleases God. Epaphras reported that the Colossians' love was genuine, and it was a powerful testimony.

Colossians 1:9

"For this cause we also, since the day we heard it, do not cease to pray for you, and to desire that ye might be filled with the knowledge of his will in all wisdom and spiritual understanding."

PAUL'S PRAYER FOR THE COLOSSIANS

Even though he hadn't met them personally, he was moved to pray for them because they had become believers and were faithfully serving the Lord. The prayer he offered is profound, and we should also pray it for ourselves and new believers.

1. Prayer to Know God's Will

"Ye might be filled with the knowledge of his will"
He wanted them to understand God's plan or will for their lives. As Christians, knowing God's will is fundamental to living a successful and purposeful life. We need to be aware of God's direction, His choices, and His divine purpose for us.

God's plan is the best plan we could ever have. "Who hath saved us, and called us with an holy calling, not according to our works, but according to his own purpose and grace, which was given us in Christ Jesus before the world began" (2 Timothy 1:9).

God's Grace and His Plan Are Interconnected
When you discover God's will for your life, you tap into His grace. Personally, I've learned that following God's plan always brings His divine help and provision. When I pursue God's path for my life, His grace comes effortlessly.

For example, if I ask someone to buy a car for me, I will provide the money needed because it's my plan. In the same way, when you walk in God's will, He supplies all you need. You won't have to struggle or beg; His provision comes naturally.

Jesus exemplified this. He said, "The Son can do nothing of himself, but what he seeth the Father do: for what things soever he doeth, these also doeth the Son likewise (John 5:19). "I can of mine own self do nothing: as I hear, I judge: and my judgment is just; because I seek not mine own will, but the will of the Father which hath sent me" (John 5:30). Jesus followed the Father's will in everything He did, and we must do the same.

How Can You Know the Will of God?

Paul's prayer that the Colossians would know God's will brings up an important question: How do we know what God's will is?

   a. *The Will of God Is Revealed by His Word*

The primary way God reveals His will is through His Word. As you read the Bible, you align yourself with God's plan. Daily reading of the Bible is crucial because it shows us what God desires for our lives.

Jesus' life was about fulfilling God's will as outlined in Scripture. "Wherefore when he cometh into the world, he saith, Sacrifice and offering thou wouldest not, but a body hast thou prepared me: In burnt offerings and sacrifices for sin thou hast had no pleasure. Then said I, Lo, I come (in the volume of the book it is written of me,) to do thy will, O God" (Hebrews 10:5-7).

We must not only read the Word but also endeavor to obey and do what it says. Sometimes people want to make sacrifices for God while neglecting to obey Him. They think giving a large offering can substitute for disobedience to His Word. But the Bible reminds us that, "Behold, to obey is better than sacrifice" (1 Samuel 15:22). True blessing comes from obedience, not just offerings. If you want to experience God's grace and provision, you must obey His Word.

   b. *The Will of God Is Revealed by the Holy Spirit*

The Holy Spirit speaks to us, showing us God's desires and leading us into all truth. Jesus said, "Howbeit when he, the Spirit of truth, is come, he will guide you into all truth" (John 16:13). The Holy Spirit not only illuminates God's Word but also highlights the Scriptures that are relevant to your specific situation. It's possible to read the Bible and miss what God is saying to you, but the Holy Spirit ensures you focus on what matters most at that moment.

These are the kinds of prayers we should also pray for ourselves and others.

The Holy Spirit Revealed My Ministry

One unforgettable experience was when I was praying in my room, and an angel appeared. This angel took my hand, and together we went up high into the sky. He placed me on a tall mast, and then he said, "God wants you to speak from here. He wants you to speak to the nations."

As I sat there, I started to speak, and I saw people being healed and transformed. I witnessed towns and entire communities being changed. The Lord told me, "This is what you have to do." That vision was the birth of my radio and TV broadcast ministry (Air Power), which now reaches over 60 countries worldwide in different languages. It's not something I do just because others are doing it. I'm doing it because it's God's plan for my life. When you follow God's specific plan for you, you will succeed.

Paul also followed God's plan for his life. He had a vision of a man from Macedonia pleading, "Come over into Macedonia, and help us" (Acts 16:9). That vision led Paul to spread the Gospel in Europe, demonstrating the importance of following divine direction.

I encourage you today: Follow God's plan for your life, as revealed through Scripture and the Holy Spirit. As Paul said, make it a prayer point: "Lord, show me Your will."

2. Prayer for Wisdom to Implement the Will of God

"In all wisdom"

Paul didn't stop at praying for them to know God's will; he also prayed for them to have wisdom. Wisdom is crucial because it's the ability to apply what you know to achieve the intended results. "The tongue of the wise useth knowledge aright" (Proverbs 15:2). You might have knowledge about something but lack the wisdom to apply it effectively.

Wisdom is about taking what you know and using it to create tangible outcomes. When people saw Jesus, they marveled, saying, "What wisdom is this, that even mighty works are wrought by his hands?" (Mark 6:2). Many people have dreams and visions but never see them come to life because they lack wisdom.

How I Started My First Building Project
One day, as I was reading Proverbs 6:6, "Go to the ant, thou sluggard; consider her ways, and be wise," the Holy Spirit gave me a revelation. At the time, I was 19 years old and still a student. God told me I was going to build a house, but I needed to build like an ant—bit by bit.

I didn't even own a piece of land. But the Holy Spirit reminded me that the ant builds little by little, carrying one grain of sand at a time until it constructs a massive anthill. I didn't have land, but God said to start with what I could. That very day, I bought a light switch. It might sound strange, but it was my first step of faith.

Over the next seven years, I kept building bit by bit, and eventually, I completed a seven-bedroom house. God provided, and the project was completed. It all began with that one small act of faith, guided by God's wisdom.

Whatever vision God gives you, ask Him for wisdom. Pray for it, because it will come in the form of ideas that may seem simple or even insignificant, but they are divine instructions.

3. Prayer for Spiritual Understanding

"Spiritual understanding"
Understanding means knowing the meaning, nature, and cause of things, especially in the spiritual realm. Sometimes, things in the natural world have a spiritual significance. "For the invisible things of him from the creation of the world are clearly seen, being understood by the things that are made, even his eternal power and Godhead" (Romans 1:20). Nature itself can teach us about God, but without spiritual insight, we miss these lessons.

We need spiritual understanding to see beyond the surface. It's not enough to observe; we must discern the spiritual meaning behind what we see. That's why Paul prayed for spiritual understanding—to help the Colossians, and us today, interpret life through God's perspective. It means that our spiritual eyes and ears must be open to perceive what God is revealing.

The Gift of a Centre Table
Before I got married, an aunt of mine, Elizabeth Heward-Mills, came to my house and gave me a living room centre table as

a gift. At the time, I was a student and didn't even have a house, so my first thought was to sell the table and use the money for something fun! But as I reflected, the Holy Spirit spoke to me: "You've received this centre table because it's time for you to get married."

That revelation changed everything. I started preparing for marriage, and not long after, I was married in my twenties. It all started with that sign and the spiritual understanding to recognize it.

Spiritual understanding is crucial. Without it, you'll miss divine signs and directions. We need revelation to navigate life effectively. "Eye hath not seen, nor ear heard, neither have entered into the heart of man, the things which God hath prepared for them that love him. But God hath revealed them unto us by his Spirit" (1 Corinthians 2:9-10). Revelation brings clarity where there was once darkness. It's like light illuminating a room, allowing you to see clearly.

I pray that God will give you the revelation you need. Whether it relates to whom to marry, how to handle a crisis, or how to deal with enemies, we need spiritual insight. May God bless us with spiritual understanding, in Jesus' name.

Colossians 1:10

"That ye might walk worthy of the Lord unto all pleasing, being fruitful in every good work, and increasing in the knowledge of God."

THE REASONS FOR PAUL'S PRAYER

1. To Please the Lord

"Walk worthy of the Lord"
Walking worthy means living in a way that pleases God. You can follow your own plans, but the way to truly please God is by following His plans. Even Jesus said, "I do always those things that please him" (John 8:29).

Why I Became a Pastor
I never wanted to be a pastor. My family background was in business, and I planned to be an architect and go into business.

But one night, while praying on the rooftop of my father's house, Jesus appeared to me. The sky lit up like daylight, and He said, "I have called you to be a teacher of God's Word and a prophet." From that moment, I knew God's will for my life. Everything I do now revolves around those two central missions. And as I follow God's will, I find that I please Him.

When we please God, heaven responds to our prayers. "Thou art my beloved Son; in thee I am well pleased" (Luke 3:22).

2. To Be Fruitful

"Being fruitful in every good work"
What are good works? They include serving in ministry, helping others, and living a righteous life. Jesus was described as one who went about "doing good" (Acts 10:38)—healing the sick and teaching God's Word.

A Baby After 15 Years of Marriage
There was a man who had been married for 15 years without a child. People pressured him to have a child outside of his marriage, but he came to church. I laid hands on him and prayed, and shortly after, his wife became pregnant. Now they have a beautiful baby girl. That's the power of doing good works through God's will. Instead of living selfishly or causing harm, we can bring blessings and hope to others.

Another example of good works is the story of Tabitha, or Dorcas, in Acts 9:36-39. She was known for her kindness and charity, making clothes for the poor. Even working honestly to provide for your family is a good work. "If any would not work, neither should he eat" (2 Thessalonians 3:10).

Whether you're a businessperson, a teacher, or a nurse, as long as you're doing honest work, you're fulfilling God's will and doing good.

3. To Know God More

"Increasing in the knowledge of God"
When we read God's Word, seek His wisdom, and gain spiritual understanding, our relationship with Him deepens. "Grow in

grace, and in the knowledge of our Lord and Saviour Jesus Christ" (2 Peter 3:18). Knowing God isn't just about reading the Bible; it's about understanding and applying His Word to our lives.

Colossians 1:11
"Strengthened with all might, according to his glorious power, unto all patience and longsuffering with joyfulness."

PAUL CONTINUES HIS REASONS FOR HIS PRAYER

1. To Walk in God's Power

"Strengthened with all might"

This spiritual strength is the miraculous power that comes from following God's will. True spiritual strength might come when you align with God's plans.

For instance, when people question why pastors don't heal every sick person in the hospital, it shows a lack of understanding. We don't act on our own will but on God's. Jesus performed miracles because He knew the Father's will. I've seen miracles myself, but they always happen according to God's will.

Some time back, I was ministering, and the Holy Spirit told me there was a blind man sitting at the back. I went to him, and when I prayed, his sight was restored instantly. Why? Because it was God's will.

2. To Walk in Patience

"Unto all patience"

Patience, or endurance, the ability to endure hardship, is another benefit of knowing God's will. Sometimes what seems like a setback is actually working for your good. The Bible reminds us to bear the weaknesses of others. "We then that are strong ought to bear the infirmities of the weak, and not to please ourselves" (Romans 15:1).

Jesus endured the cross because He knew the glory that awaited Him. When you know God's will, you can endure challenges with hope and exhibit patience.

3. To Be Filled with Joy and Longsuffering

"Longsuffering with joyfulness"

It's one thing to suffer, but it's another to do so joyfully. In Acts 27, Paul was in a storm, yet he encouraged everyone to be of good cheer because an angel had assured him of their safety. When you know God's will, even storms can't take away your joy.

My Experience

I remember being transferred from a growing church I had pastored for years to a small church. It felt like starting over. One night, Jesus appeared to me and said, "I have brought you here to make you more effective and to bless you." That revelation gave me peace and joy. Looking back, I see how God has used that move for greater impact.

Colossians 1:12

"Giving thanks unto the Father, which hath made us meet to be partakers of the inheritance of the saints in light."

REASONS FOR THANKSGIVING

You may also want to thank God for the same reasons.

1. Thanksgiving for an Inheritance

"Hath made us meet to be partakers of the inheritance of the saints in light"

God has made us qualified or helped us to meet the criteria because of the shed blood of Jesus, which allows us to partake of the spiritual inheritance reserved for His children. There are conditions attached to this.

a. You Must Be "A Saint"

The word saint means to be holy. Holiness is a change that occurs from within us. Some people seek change from the outside, but remember, change starts from the inside, not the outside.

For example, if you're looking for money, the change will come from within, not from external sources.

b. You Must Be "In the Light"

The second key to partake in God's inheritance is to be in the light. You must follow God's Word. "Thy word is a lamp unto my feet, and a light unto my path" (Psalm 119:105).

There are many people who are saints, born again, but they don't walk in the light. They don't follow God's Word. If you live like that, you won't be a successful Christian. You may have occasional breakthroughs, but you won't have consistent breakthroughs. "And he shall be like a tree planted by the rivers of water, that bringeth forth his fruit in his season; his leaf also shall not wither; and whatsoever he doeth shall prosper" (Psalm 1:3).

You must focus on obedience—consistent obedience, and then you will experience God's will. This doesn't mean you won't have problems. Problems come to everybody, but life is always better with God than without God.

Colossians 1:13

"Who hath delivered us from the power of darkness, and hath translated us into the kingdom of his dear Son."

REASONS FOR THANKSGIVING continued

You may also want to thank God for the same reasons.

2. Thanksgiving for Deliverance

"Who hath delivered us from the power of darkness"

Jesus said, "Behold, I give unto you power to tread on serpents and scorpions, and over all the power of the enemy" (Luke 10:19). Satan has power, but God is more powerful. I have personally witnessed the power of the devil firsthand.

The Woman Who Levitated

I remember one day I was ministering somewhere, and there was a large woman who came forward. When I saw her, I knew she was heavily possessed by demons. I laid hands on her, and she fell to the ground. But when she fell, something extraordinary happened—her whole body levitated about three or four inches in the air. I had never seen anything like that before. Even the ushers ran away—it was the first time I saw ushers flee! I was looking at the power of the devil.

The devil has power, and sometimes, as a minister, you can see it. But the Bible says that if you are born again and walk in the light, God will deliver you from the powers of darkness.

Don't say, "There are curses in my family," or "Things aren't working because of witches in my background." Jesus is also in your background. You are connected to Him, and the blood of Christ is greater than any curse that may be following you or your family. Focus on your spiritual lineage, not your biological lineage.

3. Thanksgiving for Transference into His Kingdom

"Translated us into the kingdom of his dear Son"

The word "translated" means He has transferred us into His Kingdom. In the realm of the spirit, there are two kingdoms: the kingdom of the devil and the Kingdom of God. A kingdom is a place or domain ruled by a king. When we are born again, the Bible says there is a spiritual transfer. We are transferred from the kingdom of darkness into the Kingdom of His dear Son. Christ becomes our King, and He rules over us.

Who Rules Over You Is Important

The person who rules over you is very important. It even shows in the country you live in. If you live in a country with good leadership, you'll have good roads, water, and development. But in a country with bad leadership, you'll have potholes on roads, poverty, and chaos.

Let's thank God for the person who rules over us—His name is Jesus. We have a good leader. The Bible talks about the leadership of Jesus: "For unto us a child is born, unto us a son is given: and the government shall be upon his shoulder: and his name shall be called Wonderful, Counsellor, The mighty God, The everlasting Father, The Prince of Peace. Of the increase of his government and peace there shall be no end" (Isaiah 9:6-7).

In the Bible, names were used to describe what someone would do. For example, Abraham means "exalted father," and he became the father of many nations. Isaiah describes Jesus' mission: Wonderful means miracles, Counsellor means He will advise you,

Everlasting Father means He will care for you, and Prince of Peace means He will bring you peace. The more He governs us, the more peace we have. Peace is one of the greatest things God can ever give you.

Always Choose Peace

Recently, I was talking to a friend of mine who is a businessman, and I said to him, "In your business, always aim for peace. Peace is better than money. Don't do business that doesn't bring you peace." "Better is an handful with quietness, than both the hands full with travail and vexation of spirit" (Ecclesiastes 4:6).

I would choose peace over a billion dollars. If you put a billion dollars in front of me but it comes with trouble, I don't want it. I want peace. The reason is simple: Without peace, you can't enjoy anything—not your marriage, your life, your sleep, your food, or anything else. What's the use?

Let's thank Him for His leadership, which brings peace.

Colossians 1:14

"In whom we have redemption through his blood, even the forgiveness of sins."

REASONS FOR THANKSGIVING continued

You may also want to thank God for the same reasons.

4. Thanksgiving for Redemption

"We have redemption through his blood"
Redemption means to pay a ransom.

The Woman Who Was Kidnapped

I had a church member from another country whose mother was kidnapped. The kidnappers demanded a ransom, and the family had to pay money for her release. After she was freed, she was so traumatized that she came to Ghana and stayed here for about six months before she could return to her country. They had to pay money for her release—that's the ransom.

The Currency in the Spirit Realm Is Blood
In the spirit realm, they don't use silver and gold. Peter says, "Forasmuch as ye know that ye were not redeemed with corruptible things, as silver and gold, from your vain conversation received by tradition from your fathers; but with the precious blood of Christ" (1 Peter 1:18-19). In the spirit realm, the currency used is blood. That's why people in the occult use blood—whether from animals, humans, or other sources.

Jesus paid for our sins with His blood and released us from the control of the enemy. Imagine your debts have been paid. That's something to thank God for—redemption. The ransom has been paid.

Colossians 1:15

"Who is the image of the invisible God, the firstborn of every creature."

WHO IS JESUS?

The Colossians believed in elemental gods. When we say elemental, we're talking about gods of nature. Some people believe that rivers, trees, stars, etc., can be gods. Those are elemental gods, gods of nature. Paul had to explain who Jesus was. Do you know who Jesus is? Let's delve in.

1. He Is the Image of God

"Image of the invisible God"
Jesus is the exact replica of God, the Father. "In the beginning God created the heaven and the earth" (Genesis 1:1). Let me use an analogy. Let's say God the Father is the sun. Jesus is the rays or brightness that you see, and the Holy Spirit is the heat that you feel. Now, which one is the sun? They are all the sun but uniquely different.

If you read the book of Hebrews, you'll see a similar thing. This is how Paul describes Jesus: "Who being the brightness of his glory, and the express image of his person, and upholding all things by the word of his power" (Hebrews 1:3). The word "glory" in Greek means "apparent" or "appearance." It's saying that when you see Jesus, you are seeing God. He is the brightness of His glory.

It's important to know God as the Creator of the universe. It helps you to tap into the creative power of God. It affects your prayer life. The Bible says, "Thou sendest forth thy spirit, they are created: and thou renewest the face of the earth" (Psalm 104:30). This knowledge is very important. Let me give you an example.

My First Experience of a Creative Miracle

Somebody gave birth to a baby, and the baby had one leg. This person said to me, "Let's go to the hospital and pray for this baby." When I went to the hospital and saw the baby, my heart sunk—one perfect leg, one deformed leg. But I said to the father, "Don't worry. We serve a God of creation. Jesus is God. He created the earth." So I said, "We are going to pray that God will give this baby a brand-new leg, a creative miracle." So we prayed. When we prayed, the leg was still the same; nothing had changed. But I continued encouraging the father, saying, "Don't worry; God will do it."

We stepped out of the ward and stood outside for a while. After about 30 minutes, we heard the nurses shouting. We came back to the ward and looked at the baby. Do you know what happened? The deformed leg had disappeared and had been replaced by a brand-new leg. It was like someone came and removed the bad leg and put a brand-new one there.

I saw a creative miracle with my own eyes. But the reason I could believe in God for that was because I believed Jesus is the Creator of the universe. He is the image of God. When I was praying in His name, I knew I was talking to the God of creation, the One who created everything. He said, "Let there be light," and there was light (Genesis 1:3).

You may think it's just a trivial statement that Jesus is the image of God, but it affects your faith and your prayer life. That's the first thing Paul said I want you to know.

2. He Is the Firstborn of Creation

"The firstborn of every creature"

The word "creature" means "creation." He's not talking about the fact that Jesus was born in Genesis. He's talking about the fact that He's the first person to get to heaven. He came to the earth, walked as a man, died, conquered death, resurrected, and went to heaven. And so He's the first man to get to heaven. And you know what? He's waiting for us to join Him. That's why we call Him the firstborn of creation.

When God created the world, it was perfect until sin came in. Now the whole world is waiting for the restoration of all things, including human beings, to their original state. He is the one "Whom the heaven must receive until the times of restitution of all things" (Acts 3:21). That word "restitution" means "restoration." He is there in heaven with a supernatural body. He's the firstborn of creation.

Paul said, "For we know that the whole creation groaneth and travaileth in pain together until now" (Romans 8:22). The time will come when even the earth will be reborn. In the book of Revelation, John said, "And I saw a new heaven and a new earth" (Revelation 21:1). Everything will be reborn. We will go back to the original state in the Garden of Eden.

Colossians 1:16

"For by him were all things created, that are in heaven, and that are in earth, visible and invisible, whether they be thrones, or dominions, or principalities, or powers: all things were created by him, and for him."

WHO IS JESUS? continued

3. He Is the Creator of All Things

"For by him were all things created"

In Paul's time, Emperor Julius Caesar claimed to be a god. The Roman emperors called themselves gods. Paul was reminding them that there is a King of kings. Jesus is the Creator of the following: Heaven, earth, visible or physical, invisible or natural, the spiritual, earth, and the natural. He also created various levels of power and authority. "Thrones" means the seat of a king. "Dominions" means masters or rulers. "Principalities" means first in rank. These show different levels of power both in the natural world and the spiritual realm.

For example, the Bible says, "Let every soul be subject unto the higher powers. For there is no power but of God: the powers that be are ordained of God" (Romans 13:1). The word "ordained" means arranged. And when it says "power," it's talking about a throne. When Paul was writing to Titus, he made a reference to it: "Put them in mind to be subject to principalities and powers, to obey magistrates, to be ready to every good work" (Titus 3:1).

This simply means God arranged a structure of authority for men: fathers, pastors, presidents, etc. The reason for this is to create social harmony and peace. "I exhort therefore, that, first of all, supplications, prayers, intercessions, and giving of thanks, be made for all men; For kings, and for all that are in authority; that we may lead a quiet and peaceable life in all godliness and honesty. For this is good and acceptable in the sight of God our Saviour" (1 Timothy 2:1-3).

A note of caution: God created the structure, or the seat of authority, but a wrong person can occupy the seat. That is why you cannot say every president or leader was appointed by God. For example, God gave Adam authority over the world, but Satan deceived him, and he now rules the world. There is a wrong person sitting on the seat God created. It would be absurd to say every husband was appointed by God.

How do we apply this to our lives? When we know that there is a God who is above all forms of power, we won't be afraid of men. "The fear of man bringeth a snare: but whoso putteth his trust in the LORD shall be safe" (Proverbs 29:25). When you know that your boss has a Boss, even when he threatens you, you will still feel secure because you know that your Boss, who is God, will not disappoint you.

I want to pray with you in case you are facing problems at work. I pray that the God of heaven, the One who is the Boss of thrones, dominions, principalities, and powers, will step in like He stepped in for Daniel and protected him.

> *Colossians 1:17*
> *"And he is before all things, and by him all things consist."*

WHO IS JESUS? continued

4. He Created All Things

"He is before all things"

This means He created all things. That's why when you read the book of Genesis 1:1, it says, "In the beginning God created the heaven and the earth."

Scientists have something called the law of singularity and the Big Bang Theory to describe how the world came into being. They suggest there was a particle somewhere in the universe, and one day some forces built up in that particle, causing it to explode, creating all the other planets.

I believe they're getting close to the truth. That singular entity they're talking about is God. And that explosion? That's when God said, "Let there be light," and there was light (Genesis 1:3). Creation began, and the whole universe was formed. He is before all things because He created all things.

Do you need a creative miracle? Believe in Him. Maybe you need a new kidney. Pray for a new kidney. Maybe you need a new eye. Pray for a new eye. "Thou sendest forth thy spirit, they are created: and thou renewest the face of the earth" (Psalm 104:30).

Miracle of Sickle Cell Status Changed

I remember a miracle testimony from someone who was sickle cell positive. After prayer, his skin changed to the skin of a newborn baby. He later went for a test, and it confirmed he was sickle cell negative. Up to today, he experienced a creative miracle.

Let's Pray for Creative Miracles

Father, in Jesus' name, I pray for anyone reading this book. I pray for the power of creation to be released. For those believing You for a creative miracle—a new heart, a new kidney, whatever it is—I pray, Lord, let Your healing hand give them new body parts. In Jesus' mighty name. Amen.

5. He Holds Everything Together

"By him all things consist"

The word "consist" means "held together." It's amazing how the planets rotate around the sun with such precision. It's amazing how there is order in the universe. Someone must be holding all these things together. "And God saw everything that he had made, and, behold, it was very good" (Genesis 1:31). Everything works together in perfect harmony, put together by God Himself. What an awesome God we serve!

Maybe there's something in your life that's not put together. Maybe it's your marriage, your business, or something else. I want you to know that God can put everything together and make it work. "The blessing of the LORD, it maketh rich, and he addeth no sorrow with it" (Proverbs 10:22).

I pray that God will put every part of your life together. If He can put the universe together, He can arrange your life—your education, your marriage, your children, your future, your spiritual life, your eternity, your finances. He can put everything together. I pray that God will bless you with a wonderful life.

Colossians 1:18

"And he is the head of the body, the church: who is the beginning, the firstborn from the dead."

WHO IS JESUS? continued

6. He Is the Head of the Church

"He is the head of the body"

The church of God is not the head of the church; Jesus is. When He was leaving the earth, He delegated that responsibility to the Holy Spirit. The Bible says, "And not holding the Head, from which all the body by joints and bands having nourishment ministered, and knit together, increaseth with the increase of God" (Colossians 2:19).

That is why we must be led by the Holy Spirit. If there is a ranking in Christianity, it is number one, the Holy Spirit; number two, the church and its ministers. But the church is under the Holy Spirit. This is why we must be obedient to the Holy Spirit.

The Bible says, "The former treatise have I made, O Theophilus, of all that Jesus began both to do and teach, Until the day in which he was taken up, after that he through the Holy Ghost had given commandments unto the apostles whom he had chosen" (Acts 1:1-2).

As soon as Jesus ascended, He delegated His authority to the Holy Spirit as the head of the church. That's why before Jesus left the earth He told His disciples, "I have yet many things to say unto you, but ye cannot bear them now. Howbeit when he, the Spirit of truth, is come, he will guide you into all truth: for he shall not speak of himself; but whatsoever he shall hear, that shall he speak: and he will shew you things to come" (John 16:12-13). Jesus said the Spirit of truth would guide us and represent Him.

Your pastor is not the head of the church. You are not the head of the church. The head of the church is the Holy Spirit. Always remember that. In terms of obedience, we must obey the Holy Spirit. Of course, the Holy Spirit works through people—apostles, prophets, evangelists, pastors, and teachers. He uses them as vessels, but they are just vessels. The head remains the Holy Spirit.

It's like being the boss of a company with an assistant managing director. The assistant acts on your behalf, but that doesn't make them the head. As pastors, we are supposed to receive instructions from the Holy Spirit.

If you want to have a successful Christian life, always listen to the voice of the Holy Spirit. The Holy Spirit will guide you, even in your role in the church and everything else.

7. He Is the First Person to Be Resurrected

"He is the beginning, first born from the dead"

Before Jesus, no one had been resurrected and gone to heaven with their body. All the people who died before Him had their bodies decomposed. The Bible says He's the firstborn from the dead, the first person to go to heaven with His body. One day, all people who are dead will be resurrected.

The Bible says, "If in this life only we have hope in Christ, we are of all men most miserable. But now is Christ risen from the dead, and become the firstfruits of them that slept" (1 Corinthians 15:19-20). The term "firstfruits" is significant. In those days, when a farmer saw the first fruit of their crop, it was a sign of a bigger harvest to come.

Similarly, when Jesus resurrected from the dead, He was the firstfruit, a sign that one day all Christians will be resurrected and be with God. Paul says, "But every man in his own order: Christ the firstfruits; afterward they that are Christ's at his coming" (1 Corinthians 15:23). This shows us how the resurrection will take place: Christ is the first to rise, followed by those who belong to Him. That's awesome.

I'm believing God for my resurrection one day. Whether I'm alive when Jesus comes or not, I'm looking forward to the resurrection. This body will be changed—no more sickness, no more weakness. What an awesome God!

8. He Is the First in All Things

"That in all things he might have the preeminence"
The word "preeminence" means He's first in all things. He's the first person to die and resurrect. He's the first person to go to heaven. That's Jesus: first in all things.

Colossians 1:19

"For it pleased the Father that in him should all fulness dwell."

WHO IS JESUS? continued

9. Everything Can Be Found in Him

"In him should all fulness dwell"
The word "fullness" means completion. When you find Jesus, you have everything: eternity, salvation, peace, a job, deliverance, money, a future, and resurrection from the dead. "But seek ye first the kingdom of God, and his righteousness; and all these things shall be added unto you" (Matthew 6:33). Wise men look for Jesus. Don't look for sex; look for Jesus. Don't look for money; look for Jesus. When you find Jesus, He will supply all your needs.

Colossians 1:20

"And, having made peace through the blood of his cross, by him to reconcile all things unto himself; by him, I say, whether they be things in earth, or things in heaven."

WHAT THE BLOOD OF JESUS HAS DONE FOR US

1. The Blood Makes Peace Between Us and God

"Having made peace through the blood of his cross"

I Was Punished in Place of My Twin Brother
While in secondary school, I experienced this concept in a powerful way. I have a twin brother, and he had done something to offend a senior student. The senior mistook me for my brother and decided to punish me. Though I protested, he didn't believe me. Later, when I told my twin about the incident, he laughed and admitted he was the one who had offended the senior. I had paid the price for his disobedience. This is what Jesus did for us. He paid the ransom, taking the punishment we deserved, so we could have peace with God. The punishment brought peace.

His blood makes peace between us and God. "In whom we have redemption through his blood, the forgiveness of sins, according to the riches of his grace" (Ephesians 1:7). The word "redemption" means to pay a ransom. In the spirit realm, the currency is not dollars or pounds; it is blood. "Forasmuch as ye know that ye were not redeemed with corruptible things, as silver and gold, but with the precious blood of Christ, as of a lamb without blemish and without spot" (1 Peter 1:18-19).

According to God's law, the punishment for sin is death. Adam and Eve sinned, and they died—separated from God. But Jesus paid the debt we owed. He died on the cross for us, paying the ransom with His blood. That's why there is now peace between us and God.

2. The Blood Reconciles Us to God

"To reconcile all things unto himself"
The word "reconcile" means to bring harmony or peace. The blood of Jesus reconciles all things to God—not just humans, but also heaven and earth. Creation itself awaits redemption "For we know that the whole creation groaneth and travaileth in pain together until now" (Romans 8:22). In the new heaven and new earth, everything will be different. Even animals and plants will change. "And I saw a new heaven and a new earth: for the first heaven and the first earth were passed away; and there was no more sea" (Revelation 21:1).

Colossians 1:21

"And you, that were sometime alienated and enemies in your mind by wicked works, yet now hath he reconciled."

WHAT THE BLOOD OF JESUS HAS DONE FOR US continued

3. Our Minds Are Renewed

"Alienated and enemies in your mind"
In other words, we were enemies of God in our minds. "Because the carnal mind is enmity against God: for it is not subject to the law of God, neither indeed can be" (Romans 8:7). That's why unbelievers don't like Christians. In their minds, they're enemies. They laugh at Christians, detest them, and even persecute them because their minds are alienated from God. Their minds are controlled by the devil. That's why unbelievers criticize pastors, insult them, and say all kinds of things. What they don't know is that there is a spirit controlling their minds.

The Bible says, "And you hath he quickened, who were dead in trespasses and sins; Wherein in time past ye walked according to the course of this world, according to the prince of the power of the air, the spirit that now worketh in the children of disobedience: Among whom also we all had our conversation in times past in the lusts of our flesh, fulfilling the desires of the flesh and of the mind; and were by nature the children of wrath, even as others" (Ephesians 2:1-3).

There is an invisible force that works on the minds of those who don't know God, and Paul says that one thing the blood did was reconcile us. It broke the power of that evil force.

4. The Blood Stopped Our Wicked Works

"By wicked works"

When Paul talks about our works, he's referring to the flesh. "Now the works of the flesh are manifest, which are these: "Adultery, fornication, uncleanness, lasciviousness, Idolatry, witchcraft, hatred, variance, emulations, wrath, strife, seditions, heresies, Envyings, murders, drunkenness, revellings, and such like: of the which I tell you before, as I have also told you in time past, that they which do such things shall not inherit the kingdom of God" (Galatians 5:19-21)

The flesh desires all kinds of evil things, from sexual immorality to divisions and occult practices. But the Bible says that when Jesus came, He broke the power of sin and our evil works. That's the power of the blood of Jesus.

Colossians 1:22

"In the body of his flesh through death, to present you holy and unblameable and unreproveable in his sight."

GOD RECONCILED US TO HIMSELF THROUGH DEATH

"In the body of his flesh through death"

He brought us together, through death. "For the wages of sin is death; but the gift of God is eternal life through Jesus Christ our Lord" (Romans 6:23). It's like owing a million dollars and someone comes and says, "I'll pay it." As soon as they pay, you're free. But in this case, the debt was not money; it was death itself. Jesus said, "I'll pay."

As soon as He paid the price, you and I were free. We don't have to die again. That's why spiritually, we are not dead or cut off from God. And when we die, we'll be resurrected because the price has been paid.

WHAT THE BLOOD OF JESUS HAS DONE FOR US continued

5. The Blood of Jesus Makes You Holy

"To present you holy and unblameable and unreproveable in his sight"

He uses three adjectives to describe this: holy, unblameable, and unreproveable. First, the blood makes you holy. It washed away your sins. Second, it made you unblameable—your conscience can't blame you for past errors. Third, you become unreproveable—your conscience cannot criticize you.

I once saw the power of the blood when I saw a converted murderer of many people preaching with a very clear conscience. Maybe you impregnated someone and denied it; but now that you are born again you can't be blamed.

God is not blaming you for anything. Why? Because it's a gift. In God's sight, you are clean.

Colossians 1:23

"If ye continue in the faith grounded and settled, and be not moved away from the hope of the gospel, which ye have heard, and which was preached to every creature which is under heaven; whereof I Paul am made a minister."

NOTHING SHOULD MOVE US AWAY FROM THE HOPE OF THE GOSPEL

The hope of the Gospel is the restoration of man to his original purpose: fellowship with God, the new Jerusalem, a new heaven and earth, and a new body.

To experience this, we must do the following:

1. Continue in Faith

"If ye continue in the faith grounded and settled"

Paul makes an important point. All the reconciliation and benefits that Jesus' blood has provided are based on one condition—you must continue in the faith. Some people get born again but then abandon the faith. Our continued enjoyment of God's blessings is connected to continuing in the faith. It's like saying, "If you want to keep receiving a salary, you must keep working." If you don't continue, you lose the benefits.

You Can Lose Your Salvation

"For it is impossible for those who were once enlightened, and have tasted of the heavenly gift, and were made partakers of the Holy Ghost, And have tasted the good word of God, and the powers of the world to come, If they shall fall away, to renew them again unto repentance; seeing they crucify to themselves the Son of God afresh, and put him to an open shame" (Hebrews 6:4-6). This is a serious warning. Many people think, "I gave my life to Christ, so I can live however I want." That's a deception from the pit of hell.

"And if any man shall take away from the words of the book of this prophecy, God shall take away his part out of the book of life, and out of the holy city, and from the things which are written in this book" (Revelation 22:19). Can you imagine? Your name can be taken out of the Book of Life. Jesus was writing to churches, born-again believers in Ephesus, Philadelphia, Laodicea, and others when He gave this warning.

The Bible shows us that the Israelites were delivered from Egypt but couldn't enter the Promised Land because of their disobedience. "But with many of them God was not well pleased: for they were overthrown in the wilderness. Now these things were our examples, to the intent we should not lust after evil things, as they also lusted" (1 Corinthians 10:5-6).

2. You Are Not Moved from the Hope of the Gospel

"Be not moved away from the hope of the gospel"

What is the hope of the Gospel? "Christ in you, the hope of glory" (Colossians 1:27). "For all have sinned, and come short of the glory of God" (Romans 3:23). The glory that Adam had is the hope of the Gospel. Adam was a friend of God. He had no sin, he did not know poverty, he could not fall ill, he could not die, and creation was in peace and harmony till he sinned. This was before sin came into the world. One day, God will restore that glory to man, and we will be as God intended: blessed, reflecting His image, and flourishing in every way. That's the hope of the Gospel.

Colossians 1:24
"Who now rejoice in my sufferings for you, and fill up that which is behind of the afflictions of Christ in my flesh for his body's sake, which is the church."

PAUL'S TESTIMONY ABOUT HIMSELF

1. He Rejoices in His Sufferings for Them

"Rejoice in my sufferings for you"

One thing that you may have to go through as a Christian is suffering for the sake of others. The Bible says, "But let none of you suffer as a murderer, or as a thief, or as an evildoer, or as a busybody in other men's matters. Yet if any man suffer as a Christian, let him not be ashamed; but let him glorify God on this behalf" (1 Peter 4:15-16).

Sometimes as Christians, we suffer because of our faith and principles. For example, you could have a problem with a friend, but you may have to swallow your pride and apologize to make peace, even if it's your friend who provoked you. Can you do that in a marital relationship? Sometimes you might not speak to your spouse for a week due to pride. Can you swallow your pride and make up?

To Endure Suffering, You Must Focus on the Prize

Students endure sleepless nights not because they enjoy studying, but because they are focusing on the prize of becoming an engineer to earn a good salary. When you focus on the prize, suffering becomes bearable. This is what Jesus did. We must keep "looking unto Jesus the author and finisher of our faith; who for the joy that was set before him endured the cross, despising the shame, and is set down at the right hand of the throne of God" (Hebrews 12:2).

Jesus endured suffering because He focused on the prize of sitting at the right hand of God. "Consider him that endured such contradiction of sinners against himself, lest ye be wearied and faint in your minds" (Hebrews 12:3). When we focus on eternal things, suffering becomes easier. I pray that you lift up your perspective and focus on eternal things.

Colossians 1:25

"Whereof I am made a minister, according to the dispensation of God which is given to me for you, to fulfil the word of God."

PAUL'S TESTIMONY ABOUT HIMSELF continued

2. He Is a Minister for the Gospel

"I am made a minister"

The word "minister" comes from the Greek word *diakonos*, which means deacon or servant. Literally, it means "to run an errand."

In the New Testament church, there were priests and deacons. The priests handled spiritual matters, while the deacons took care of physical matters, such as sharing food and supporting the poor. Both roles are equally important. Peter said, "Wherefore, brethren, look ye out among you seven men of honest report, full of the Holy Ghost and wisdom, whom we may appoint over this business. But we will give ourselves continually to prayer, and to the ministry of the word" (Acts 6:3-4).

Sometimes people undervalue physical service, but as long as it is done for the glory of God, it is just as important as spiritual service. "Whether therefore ye eat, or drink, or whatsoever ye do, do all to the glory of God" (1 Corinthians 10:31). If even eating and drinking should glorify God, then any task can be a service to Him.

In the Old Testament, not all Levites were priests. There were only five priests in Moses' time: Aaron and his sons. The other Levites carried out physical work, like transporting the tabernacle, cleaning, and assisting with sacrifices. Today, Levites can be likened to deacons in the church, and priests to full-time ministers.

3. He Managed God's Household

"According to the dispensation of God which is given to me"
The word "dispensation" comes from the Greek word *oikonomos*, meaning "household manager." For example, Joseph managed Potiphar's household. Similarly, Paul says God's household comprises born-again Christians, and God has assigned them a specific role within it.

Paul's assignment was revealed on the road to Damascus. The Lord said to him, "I have appeared unto thee for this purpose, to make thee a minister and a witness both of these things which thou hast seen, and of those things in the which I will appear unto thee; Delivering thee from the people, and from the Gentiles, unto whom now I send thee, To open their eyes, and to turn them from darkness to light, and from the power of Satan unto God" (Acts 26:16-18). Paul's responsibility was to take God's Word to the Gentiles, open their eyes, and lead them from darkness to light.

Learn to Focus on Your Assignment
Personally, I've learned to focus on my specific assignment. I don't try to do everything. I've learned to be comfortable in my calling. If you try to do everything, you'll get tired and confused. Paul said, "I know my assignment." When you know your assignment, you can rest in the Lord. I pray the Holy Ghost will reveal your assignment to you.

4. He Wanted to Obey God's Word

"To fulfil the word of God"
When you read God's Word, it will place responsibilities: prayer, witnessing, giving, etc. The more you read it, the more accountable you are. "For unto whomsoever much is given, of him shall be much required" (Luke 12:48). We have responsibilities as fathers, friends, children, and business owners, and all are outlined in God's Word.

I pray that you will fulfil your responsibilities as revealed by the Scriptures.

> *Colossians 1:26*
> *"Even the mystery which hath been hid from ages and from generations, but now is made manifest to his saints."*

UNDERSTANDING THE MYSTERY OF GOD

1. The Mystery Has Been Revealed to Saints

'Made manifest to his saints'

The word "saint" means a holy person. Mystery means something that is difficult to understand. To understand God's mysteries and spiritual truths, you must walk in holiness.

There are many people who don't understand the Scriptures because they have not been cleansed by the blood. They are not born again, and even if they are, sin blinds them from having spiritual understanding. "In whom the god of this world hath blinded the minds of them which believe not, lest the light of the glorious gospel of Christ, who is the image of God, should shine unto them" (2 Corinthians 4:4). "Yea, the light of the wicked shall be put out, and the spark of his fire shall not shine. The light shall be dark in his tabernacle, and his candle shall be put out with him" (Job 18:5-6).

Revelation is the key to possession. When something is revealed, you will possess it. For example, you can never be born again until the Holy Spirit reveals Jesus to you, though you may attend church and read the Bible. "The secret things belong unto the LORD our God: but those things which are revealed belong unto us and to our children for ever, that we may do all the words of this law" (Deuteronomy 29:29). Pray that God reveals the mysteries of His wisdom, anointing, and grace to you and me.

WHY IT WAS A MYSTERY

1. It Was Hidden for Ages (A Long Period of Time)

"The mystery which hath been hid from ages"

The term "ages" refers to a long period of time. From the time of Adam to Paul's day. From Adam's fall to the present, people only had glimpses of God's plan. Old Testament saints didn't fully understand God's purposes. Concepts like heaven and hell were vague.

For example, the Old Testament speaks of Sheol, a divided place for the righteous and the wicked. Only when Jesus came were the realities of heaven and hell made clear, as seen in Luke 16:19-23, where Jesus describes the rich man and Lazarus.

The revelation of God in the Bible is progressive. The full truth was revealed in Christ. "God, who at sundry times and in divers manners spake in time past unto the fathers by the prophets, Hath in these last days spoken unto us by his Son" (Hebrews 1:1-2).

2. It Was Hidden from Generations of People

"From generations"
Generations of people lived without understanding this mystery.

When Adam and Eve sinned, they lost God's image and glory. God's plan to restore humanity began with the law and sacrifices, culminating in Jesus' death and resurrection. Through Christ, our spirits are reborn, our souls are being transformed, and our bodies will be glorified at the resurrection. "For all have sinned, and come short of the glory of God" (Romans 3:23).

Colossians 1:27

"To whom God would make known what is the riches of the glory of this mystery among the Gentiles; which is Christ in you, the hope of glory."

WHAT IS THIS MYSTERY?

"Christ in you, the hope of glory"
The literal meaning of glory is appearance. One day, the Kingdom of God will appear visibly to our senses. Creation will be restored to its original state. John said, "And I saw a new heaven and a new earth: for the first heaven and the first earth were passed away; and there was no more sea. And I John saw the holy city, new Jerusalem, coming down from God out of heaven, prepared as a bride adorned for her husband. And I heard a great voice out

of heaven saying, Behold, the tabernacle of God is with men, and he will dwell with them, and they shall be his people, and God himself shall be with them, and be their God. And God shall wipe away all tears from their eyes; and there shall be no more death, neither sorrow, nor crying, neither shall there be any more pain: for the former things are passed away" (Revelation 21:1-4). When Christ is in you, you have hope that you will experience this glory. This is the mystery that was hidden.

WHICH PEOPLE QUALIFY FOR THIS?

"Christ in you, the hope of glory"

Those who qualify for this have "Christ in them" or are born again. "The Spirit itself beareth witness with our spirit, that we are the children of God" (Romans 8:16). Are you born again? Remember, it's not about going to church or being a good person. It is by the Holy Spirit confirming or witnessing that you are His child. If you are not, I can show you how.

First, repent and decide to turn away from all evil. Second, pray and ask for His blood to wash away your sins. Third, confess Jesus as your Lord from today. In other words, you will obey His will as revealed in Scripture and by the Holy Spirt. Next, be baptized with water.

Colossians 1:28

"Whom we preach, warning every man, and teaching every man in all wisdom; that we may present every man perfect in Christ Jesus."

WE MUST BE READY AND PREPARED BECAUSE OF THIS HOPE

Preparation is be done with the following:

1. Preaching

"Whom we preach"

Christ must be preached. Not ourselves, our church, our country, money, or power, but Christ only. Imagine knowing a place free of suffering and difficulties. Wouldn't you want to guide your loved ones there? Paul's eternal perspective drove him to preach Christ.

Many Christians have lost this perspective, focusing only on earthly matters. Let's remember that this world is not our home. "Dearly beloved, I beseech you as strangers and pilgrims, abstain from fleshly lusts, which war against the soul" (1 Peter 2:11).

2. Warning

"Warning every man"

God's judgement is real, hell is real, the lake of fire is real, and we must warn people about it. Imagine knowing about an impending disaster and not warning your loved ones. Paul warns of judgment and emphasizes that Christ is humanity's only hope.

Are you warning others or you are only warning them about a particular stock or political party? The ultimate warning is about the consequences of sin. Share the Gospel with those around you.

3. Teaching

"Teaching every man"

Teaching helps believers maintain an eternal perspective. Without sound teaching, Christians may become fixated on earthly concerns. Teaching reminds us to prepare for Christ's return and live with eternity in mind. You can decide to teach people in your sphere of influence about Christ. You don't need a pulpit.

THE IMPORTANCE OF ALL THESE

4. To Perfect Christians

"That we may present every man perfect in Christ Jesus"

The goal is to perfect or help believers to grow spiritually and be complete. Paul encouraged the Colossians to mature in their faith and understand that their hope lies in Christ, not in worldly things like money, politics, or possessions. Spiritual maturity comes from recognizing that Christ in us, the Holy Spirit in us, is a reminder that this world is not our home and one day we will go home.

Colossians 1:29

"Whereunto I also labour, striving according to his working, which worketh in me mightily."

THE PURPOSE FOR LABORING FOR THE LORD

Why was Paul so dedicated? What was his motivation? We can learn from him.

1. The Hope of Glory

"Whereunto I also labour"

Paul said the purpose or reason for his labor was the hope of glory. Whereunto means for this purpose or reason. This has already been stated.

2. The Power of the Holy Spirit

"Striving according to his working, which worketh in me mightily"

This supernatural ability to serve and work for the Lord is not a natural gift but a divine empowerment by the Holy Spirit. "For it is God which worketh in you both to will and to do of his good pleasure" (Philippians 2:13).

The Holy Spirit Works in Us in Two Key Ways

First, he influences our will by aligning our desires with God's purposes, enabling us to choose to serve Him.

Second, he empowers our actions by providing the energy and ability to carry out God's work. Some people struggle with attending church, praying, or giving. These challenges can stem from a lack of spiritual empowerment.

Do you struggle to share God's Word with others? Maybe you feel shy or you are just plain lazy. Pray for the Holy Spirit to empower you.

COLOSSIANS CHAPTER 2

Colossians 2:1

"For I would that ye knew what great conflict I have for you, and for them at Laodicea, and for as many as have not seen my face in the flesh."

THE STRUGGLE TO PREACH THE WORD

"What great conflict I have for you"

The church in Colossae wasn't established by Paul but by Epaphras, one of his fellow workers. Paul referred to Epaphras as his "companion in labour" (Philemon 1:23). Despite not knowing them in person, Paul sought to connect with them by sharing his challenges.

Sometimes it's good to let people know what you're going through. If you don't tell them, they might form wrong impressions about you or not appreciate you.

Colossians 2:2

"That their hearts might be comforted, being knit together in love, and unto all riches of the full assurance of understanding, to the acknowledgment of the mystery of God, and of the Father, and of Christ."

WHY YOU MUST SHARE NOT ONLY YOUR VICTORIES BUT ALSO YOUR STRUGGLES

1. To Comfort Others

"That their hearts might be comforted"

There is comfort in numbers. For instance, if you fail an exam and meet a friend who also failed, it makes you feel less alone and helps to normalize it.

2. It Creates Empathy

"Being knit together in love"
If you've lost a child, failed an exam, or faced poverty, meeting someone with a similar experience fosters connection. Paul shared his struggles to strengthen their bond and unity.

3. It Gives Others Confidence

"Unto all riches of the full assurance"
If someone who was being persecuted heard that Paul received "forty stripes save one" (2 Corinthians 11:24), their trials might seem light compared to Paul's. Paul's endurance helped them stand firm in their faith.

Colossians 2:3-4

"In whom are hid all the treasures of wisdom and knowledge. And this I say, lest any man should beguile you with enticing words."

HIDDEN TREASURES IN CHRIST

1. Wisdom

"Treasures of wisdom"
There are different types of wisdom: the wisdom of the world and the wisdom of God. One major difference is that one is based on knowledge, the other on faith. "We speak wisdom among them that are perfect: yet not the wisdom of this world" (1 Corinthians 2:6). The wisdom of God is to be treasured above all. If you live long enough, you will come to the conclusion that God's Word is true because you will experience it.

2. Knowledge

"Treasures of knowledge"
You cannot make a good decision with poor information. The Word of God is full of supernatural knowledge, which helps us to make the right decisions. For example, how can you choose the

right spouse when you cannot predict the future? Application of the Word can help you to overcome this.

Colossians 2:5
"For though I be absent in the flesh,
yet am I with you in the spirit, joying and beholding your order,
and the steadfastness of your faith in Christ."

SPIRITUAL PRESENCE

1. It Is Possible to Be Spiritually Present but Physically Absent

"Yet am I with you in the spirit"

This sounds strange but possible. Our bodies are confined to one place, but our spirits are not. That is why we can be spiritually translated to the Kingdom of heaven when we become born again but physically bound to our existing location. "Who hath delivered us from the power of darkness, and hath translated us into the kingdom of his dear Son" (Colossians 1:13).

The Pastor Whose Church Was Not Growing

One day a pastor came to see me for prayer because his church was not growing. I agreed to pray with him, but as I prayed, I saw a vision. In the vision, I saw this same man with another pastor's wife. He had committed adultery with her during a visit to that pastor's church. That incident had caused a spiritual block, affecting the growth of his church.

After the prayer, I called him aside and described everything I saw. I even described the place and the event in detail. He admitted it was true and confessed his sin. I prayed with him, and he repented. I encouraged him to serve the Lord faithfully, assuring him that if his repentance was genuine, God could restore his ministry.

WHAT PAUL SAW ABOUT THEM

1. Organization

"Beholding your order"
Paul likened the church to a body that must be orderly and organized, just as the human body is. Every part of the body—eyes, ears, hands, and feet—has a specific position and function. "Now ye are the body of Christ, and members in particular. And God hath set some in the church, first apostles, secondarily prophets, thirdly teachers, after that miracles, then gifts of healings, helps, governments, diversities of tongues" (1 Corinthians 12:27-28). Every member has a unique role.

Problems arise when members try to take on roles that aren't theirs, like a toe wanting to become the brain. This isn't a corporate ladder where we "climb" to higher positions; it's a body with specialized parts working together. The goal isn't to compete but to excel in the role God has given us.

What Is Your Role in the Body of Christ?
Are you functioning in the place God has called you to? When every member of the church accepts their role and functions as intended, the body of Christ operates in unity and effectiveness.

2. Faith

"Steadfastness of your faith in Christ"
To be steadfast means to be firm and unwavering. Some people start well in their faith journey but fail to remain steadfast.

"It Was a Mistake" to Be Born Again
I remember witnessing to a man who gave his life to Christ. The very next day, I visited him for follow-up, only to find him in bed with his girlfriend. He was embarrassed, but I asked, "Didn't you just commit your life to Christ yesterday?" He replied, "Pastor, I think I made a mistake." He didn't remain steadfast in his decision for even 24 hours.

Jesus warned about this in the Parable of the Sower. "Those by the way side are they that hear; then cometh the devil, and taketh away the word out of their hearts, lest they should believe and be saved" (Luke 8:12). The devil often sows doubt to steal the Word of God from our hearts.

The Example of Adam and Eve
This is exactly what happened to Adam and Eve in the Garden of Eden. The serpent questioned God's command, saying, "Yea, hath God said, Ye shall not eat of every tree of the garden?" (Genesis 3:1). Doubt led to disobedience, which ultimately resulted in their fall.

We must remain steadfast, holding firmly to God's Word, despite challenges, doubts, or external pressures.

Colossians 2:6

"As ye have therefore received Christ Jesus the Lord, so walk ye in him."

WHAT TO DO AFTER YOU HAVE RECEIVED CHRIST

1. Grow Up Spiritually

"So walk ye in him"
Walking in Christ signifies spiritual growth. When we first come to Christ, we are spiritual babies. Babies can't walk; they move or crawl. God expects us to grow from lying down to crawling, then to walking. Spiritual maturity involves taking responsibility for others, as adults do. Paul rebuked the Hebrews, saying, "For when for the time ye ought to be teachers, ye have need that one teach you again which be the first principles of the oracles of God" (Hebrews 5:12).

If you've been a baby Christian for too long, it's time to grow. Start sharing the Word with others. It's a sign of maturity when you minister to others, whether in your family, workplace, or community.

Colossians 2:7

"Rooted and built up in him, and stablished in the faith, as ye have been taught, abounding therein with thanksgiving."

2. How to Be Established in Christ

"Rooted in him"
To be rooted means to be deeply established. A tree with deep roots can withstand strong winds, while one with shallow roots is easily uprooted.

Spiritual maturity is about being stable in God's Word. It's not about spiritual gifts, which are given instantly, but about growing in understanding and application of the Word. Gifts are not a sign of maturity. Christmas trees are erected in an instant, and they usually have gifts placed under them, but real trees grow and produce fruit over time.

One sign of growth is maturity in God's Word. "That we henceforth be no more children, tossed to and fro, and carried about with every wind of doctrine" (Ephesians 4:14). A mature Christian is not easily swayed by false teachings or doubts.

Doctrine is vital because it influences our thinking, and our thinking shapes our behavior. When doctrine is flawed, behavior becomes flawed too. For instance, you may hear teachings like, "To have your prayers answered, you must light a candle, open Psalm 91, and wear white." These are traditions and practices not rooted in the Bible.

3. You Must Develop Spiritually

"Built up in him"
There are people who have developed their muscles in the gym. In the same way, your spiritual muscles can be developed.

   a. *Prayer Builds You Up*

Aim to pray a minimum of one hour a day, and you will be spiritually developed. "But ye, beloved, building up yourselves on your most holy faith, praying in the Holy Ghost" (Jude 1:20).

Praying in tongues is a powerful tool that enhances your prayer life and opens doors to spiritual gifts and power.

b. The Word Builds You Up

"As newborn babes, desire the sincere milk of the word, that ye may grow thereby" (1 Peter 2:2). Do you feed on God's Word every day, or do you feed on social media? Read your Bible and pray every day if you want to grow.

c. Application of the Word

Spiritual growth requires more than just knowing the Word; it demands applying it. "But strong meat belongeth to them that are of full age, even those who by reason of use have their senses exercised to discern both good and evil" (Hebrews 5:14). Practice the Word of God in your home, marriage, workplace, friendships, and every area of life. Go to the "spiritual gym."

4. Be Established in Faith

"Stablished in the faith"
This means to be stable and to serve God consistently over a long time. I've been a Christian for over 30 years, and by God's grace, I've remained consistent in attending church, praying, and reading the Bible. The rewards of serving God often take time to manifest, but "they that sow in tears shall reap in joy" (Psalm 126:5).

The Example of Demas
Unfortunately, some Christians, like Demas, fail because they are not stable. Paul lamented, "For Demas hath forsaken me, having loved this present world" (2 Timothy 4:10). The lure of worldly pleasures—money, parties, and leisure—can pull people away from their faith. Others, like Judas, fell for money's deception. Judas betrayed Jesus for 30 pieces of silver, leading to his tragic end.

5. Be Full of Thanksgiving

"Abounding therein with thanksgiving"
"In everything give thanks: for this is the will of God in Christ Jesus concerning you" (1 Thessalonians 5:18). Being thankful shifts our focus from what we lack to what we have, from the natural to the spiritual, and from ourselves to God.

Sometimes you can focus on 10 percent of what is lacking in your spouse and forget the 90 percent of what you like. Same with God.

A successful marriage often depends on focusing on the good qualities of your spouse rather than their flaws. Everyone has faults, but gratitude fosters love and harmony. Even in difficult situations, we can find reasons to be thankful.

For example, someone who has experienced a miscarriage might focus on the pain of losing the baby. But by shifting perspective, they might thank God for preserving their life during the ordeal. Focusing on blessings, even in hardship, enables us to give thanks.

Start each day by thanking God. Whether it's for food, shelter, health, or the ability to work, give thanks. When we cultivate gratitude, the Holy Spirit flows freely. Complaining and murmuring, on the other hand, quench the Spirit.

Colossians 2:8

"Beware lest any man spoil you through philosophy and vain deceit, after the tradition of men, after the rudiments of the world, and not after Christ."

WARNINGS FOR CHRISTIANS

There are things that can spoil or destroy your faith in God. Let's examine them.

1. Wisdom (Philosophy)

"Lest any man spoil you through philosophy"
Philosophy means "the love of wisdom," especially the wisdom of this world. Worldly wisdom often contradicts God's wisdom.

For instance, the world says, "Retaliate when someone wrongs you," but Jesus taught, "Love your enemies, bless them that curse you" (Matthew 5:44).

I have seen people make marital choices based on worldly wisdom, and it has many times spelled disaster.

2. Deception

"Vain deceit"

Deception often comes through our senses—what we see, hear, and feel. Eve was deceived when she "saw that the tree was good for food" (Genesis 3:6). Don't trust your senses over God's Word. Many schemes look enticing, but you have to stick to God's Word, even when the world's promises seem appealing.

I have a Christian friend who did some business deals with worldly wisdom. He had to flee the country because of debts.

3. Tradition

"Tradition of men"

Traditions, whether from family, culture, or even the church, can undermine God's Word. For instance, in Jesus' time, some traditions contradicted Scripture. Jesus said, "Ye have heard that it hath been said, Thou shalt love thy neighbour, and hate thine enemy. But I say unto you, Love your enemies" (Matthew 5:43-44). He redefined teachings distorted by tradition.

Even in modern times, we encounter traditions that don't align with Scripture.

4. Principles of the World

"The rudiments of the world"

Rudiments refers to the basic principles or foundational systems of this world. Just as phonics is fundamental to learning to read (e.g., A for apple, B for ball), the world has its own fundamental principles.

One such principle is the normalization of debt. The world teaches that debt is a necessary part of life, but this principle contradicts God's Word of being content with what you have, which avoids debts. "For I have learned, in whatsoever state I am, therewith to be content" (Philippians 4:11). Many are drowning in debt because they are not content with what they can afford.

Another principle of the world is that love must always be expressed physically, often through sexual relationships, even outside of marriage. These are worldly principles that undermine God's truth.

Paul's warning is clear. Don't let these principles guide your life. Instead, let God's Word shape your thinking and actions. God's principles often lead to divine acceleration.

Colossians 2:9

"For in him dwelleth all the fulness of the Godhead bodily."

JESUS IS GOD IN THE FLESH

The "Godhead" means divinity: the attributes and qualities of God, such as holiness, power, and mercy. Fullness means completely filled up. He was not a demigod, half God and half man. He was a hundred percent God and a hundred percent man. "And the Word was made flesh, and dwelt among us" (John 1:14). Some struggle with this truth, seeing Jesus as merely a prophet or a great teacher.

Jesus wasn't just a man; He was God incarnate. This truth is foundational to the Christian faith. The greatest proof is the resurrection of the dead. "And declared to be the Son of God with power, according to the spirit of holiness, by the resurrection from the dead" (Romans 1:4).

Colossians 2:10
"And ye are complete in him, which is the head of all principality and power."

CHRIST COMPLETES US

1. Provision

"Ye are complete in him"
Complete means not lacking any necessary thing. Without Christ, you will miss many things in life and eternity. You will not be complete. Everything you need, both spiritual and material, can be found in Christ. If you have Jesus, you have everything. "He that spared not His own Son, but delivered Him up for us all, how shall He not with Him also freely give us all things?" (Romans 8:32).

Salvation Can Be Found in Jesus, Not in Good Works
You might hear someone say, "I'm a good person—I give to the poor, I don't hurt anyone." But salvation isn't in good works. Everything is in Christ. That's why you're complete in Him.

Righteousness Can Be Found in Jesus
Some people think you need to add something to Jesus to be righteous. They say things like, "Women shouldn't wear trousers," or "If you eat this, you won't go to heaven." These rules come from the Old Testament, but God's Word is progressive. In the Old Testament, they used animal sacrifices to atone for sin. But in the New Testament, it's the blood of Jesus that cleanses us. Mixing the two covenants only brings confusion.

"For Christ is the end of the law for righteousness to every one that believeth" (Romans 10:4). The "law" here means the 613 commandments of Moses. Nobody could keep them all perfectly, but Christ fulfilled them. Now, righteousness comes only through faith in Jesus' blood. Animal sacrifices are over. Forgiveness is found in Christ alone.

Material Things Can Be Found in Jesus

Jesus affirmed this when He said: "For after all these things do the Gentiles seek: for your heavenly Father knoweth that ye have need of all these things. But seek ye first the kingdom of God, and his righteousness; and all these things shall be added unto you" (Matthew 6:32-33).

2. Protection

"Which is the head of all principality and power"

Christ has all power, "And Jesus came and spake unto them, saying, All power is given unto me in heaven and in earth" (Matthew 28:18). "Principality" means first in rank, time, and authority. "Power" is the force to enforce that authority.

It doesn't matter who or what it is—a president, an evil spirit, your boss, your teacher, even your parents—Christ is above them all. "That at the name of Jesus every knee should bow, of things in heaven, and things in earth, and things under the earth" (Philippians 2:10). His authority covers heaven, earth, and hell. That's why we don't have to fear demons. "No weapon that is formed against thee shall prosper; and every tongue that shall rise against thee in judgment thou shalt condemn" (Isaiah 54:17).

Nightmares

One day I had a terrible visitation. A man walked into my room and introduced himself as Satan. My heart froze; I couldn't believe it. He was well-dressed and had a wonderful smile. I remembered Jesus was the head of all principality and power and screamed, *"Jesus!"* Straightaway he disappeared. When you have a nightmare, wake up and rebuke it in Jesus' name! At His name, every knee will bow.

Colossians 2:11

"In whom also ye are circumcised with the circumcision made without hands, in putting off the body of the sins of the flesh by the circumcision of Christ."

3. Spiritual Circumcision

"Ye are circumcised with the circumcision made without hands"
What is circumcision? In the Old Testament it was a physical sign that you were of the seed of Abraham and also in covenant with God.

God Made a Covenant with Abraham
"Now the LORD had said unto Abram, Get thee out of thy country, and from thy kindred, and from thy father's house, unto a land that I will shew thee…and in thee shall all families of the earth be blessed" (Genesis 12:1-3). To identify His people, God commanded Abraham, "Ye shall circumcise the flesh of your foreskin; and it shall be a token or physical sign of the covenant betwixt me and you" (Genesis 17:11). Circumcision was God's physical "signature" of His covenant with Abraham and his seed.

Circumcision in the New Testament Is Modified
New Testament circumcision is not physical; it's spiritual. It's not about cutting your flesh; it's about cutting off sin, "putting off the body of the sins of the flesh." Are you bitter against your spouse? Are you envious of a work colleague? Are you living with someone you are not married to? These are examples of things we must "circumcise." "I beseech you therefore, brethren, by the mercies of God, that ye present your bodies a living sacrifice, holy, acceptable unto God, which is your reasonable service" (Romans 12:1).

Holiness Is a Sign of Spiritual Circumcision
When Jesus returns, He won't ask what church you attended or if you were born again. He will be looking for His covenant sign: holiness. "Follow peace with all men, and holiness, without which no man shall see the Lord" (Hebrews 12:14).

We Are Circumcised but "Without Hands"

This means our circumcision as Christians is not done by a doctor or human effort. It's the work of the Holy Spirit, who cuts away the power of sin in your life. "They that are Christ's have crucified the flesh with the affections and lusts" (Galatians 5:24). "For if ye live after the flesh, ye shall die: but if ye through the Spirit do mortify the deeds of the body, ye shall live" (Romans 8:13).

Years ago I was reluctant to give my life to Jesus because I felt I could not live a holy life. I was relying on willpower. When I was born again, I suddenly developed the desire and strength to lead a holy life. The Holy Spirit did His work of circumcision. Maybe you are sitting on the fence of full commitment; trust the Holy Spirit to help you. He's the only One who can break sin's grip and help us live righteously.

Colossians 2:12

"Buried with him in baptism, wherein also ye are risen with him through the faith of the operation of God, who hath raised him from the dead."

THE SIGNIFICANCE OF BAPTISM

1. Baptism Is the Burial of Our Corrupted Spirit

"Buried with him in baptism"

Baptism is a burial—but if you're still alive, what part of you is being buried? Your corrupted spirit. Paul said, "That ye put off concerning the former conversation the old man, which is corrupt according to the deceitful lusts" (Ephesians 4:22). He made reference to the deceitful lists of Adam and Eve when they were tempted by the devil. Not your physical body, but the sinful, corrupt nature inside you that Paul calls "the old man." It has to be executed and buried.

A Lesson from My Late Father

Since my father died and we buried him, he has not committed a single sin. He has not been envious, quarreled with his wife, or had a single negative thought. That's what happens in spiritual burial. The "the old man," the corrupt spirit, is buried.

Because of this we don't use our bodies to serve sin but to serve God, because the "old man" cannot connive with it. "Knowing this, that our old man is crucified with Him, that the body of sin might be destroyed (disabled), that henceforth we should not serve sin" (Romans 6:6).

Think of It This Way
Your flesh is the TV; the old nature is the remote. Destroy the remote, and the TV can't be controlled by the remote anymore. The Holy Spirit, "the physical buttons" on the TV, now controls you. Water baptism is the symbolic representation of what has happened.

2. Baptism Is Symbolic of a New Life

"Ye are risen with him through faith "
Christ didn't stay buried—He rose! Spiritually we also rise from the dead because we receive a new spirit, the new man. "And that ye put on the new man, which after God is created in righteousness and true holiness" (Ephesians 4:24).

I remember after I became born again, the things of God became real to me because I was now spiritually alive and able to relate to God through my spiritual senses. I started praying, reading the Bible, and attending church and enjoying it. Physically dead people can't relate with the living; in the same way spiritually dead people cannot relate to God.

3. Baptism Makes Us Spiritually Alive

"through the faith of the operation of God, who hath raised him from the dead"
Jesus was raised from the dead by God. In the same way, we become spiritually alive to God through the operation of faith. This happens when we repent and express faith in the shed blood of Jesus, which washes away sin.

"That if thou shalt confess with thy mouth the Lord Jesus, and shalt believe in thine heart that God hath raised him from the dead, thou shalt be saved. For with the heart man believeth unto righteousness; and with the mouth confession is made unto salvation," and, "If any man be in Christ, he is a new creature: old things are passed away; behold, all things are become new" (Romans 10:9-10, 2 Corinthians 5:17).

The Bean Seed

When I was a boy, I planted a bean seed. The next day, I dug it up to see if it had changed—but it looked the same. My uncle told me, "Leave it! It needs time." Days later, when the seed died, a green shoot sprouted and was totally different from the seed I buried.

That's how it is with salvation. If you're truly born again, first you must die spiritually, and after, there should be visible change. Some Christians claim to be saved, but their old life is still there. They are still into clubbing, lying, prideful, not praying, and have no interest in the Bible. The "old man" isn't buried; he's still walking around!

But the Bible says the power of sin is broken. You can overcome porn addiction and anger because the devil's grip on your flesh is destroyed. Rise up and live as a new man in your marriage, at work, in church, etc.

Colossians 2:13

"And you, being dead in your sins and the uncircumcision of your flesh, hath he quickened together with him, having forgiven you all trespasses."

CAUSES OF SPIRITUAL DEATH

"And you, being dead in your sins and the uncircumcision of your flesh"

To be spiritually dead means you cannot relate to God because the dead do not relate to the living. Example: You don't talk to God through prayer, and God does not talk to you through His Word. What causes this? Two reasons are given.

a. Sin

"Dead in your sins"

God is holy, and sin separates us from God because we don't share His nature. Isaiah said, "But your iniquities have separated between you and your God, and your sins have hid his face from you, that he will not hear" (Isaiah 59:2). A bird and a dog can never be friends because they are totally different.

b. Circumcision

"Uncircumcision"

God told Abraham to circumcise the foreskin of his descendants because it was an outward sign of his covenant with God. In the new covenant, the sign that we are God's children is in our hearts; we are born again. "But he is a Jew, which is one inwardly; and circumcision is that of the heart, in the spirit, and not in the letter; whose praise is not of men, but of God" (Romans 2:29).

HOW TO BECOME SPIRITUALLY ALIVE

"Quickened together with him"

The word "quickened" means made spiritually alive. Before salvation, we were dead to God—unresponsive, like a corpse at a wake.

When you become born again, you come alive. Suddenly, the Bible makes sense. Worship moves you, and prayer isn't a chore anymore. If you're losing interest in spiritual things, it's a warning that you're backsliding. You have to repent and get your fire back on.

Colossians 2:14

"Blotting out the handwriting of ordinances that was against us, which was contrary to us, and took it out of the way, nailing it to his cross."

WHAT HAPPENED ON THE CROSS?

1. Curses Were Erased

"Blotting out the handwriting of ordinances"

Ordinance means a law, specifically, the law of Moses. The law contained both curses and blessings.

In Deuteronomy 28, God instructed Moses to repeat the law to Israel before entering the Promised Land. Half of the people stood on Mount Gerizim, and the other half stood on Mount Ebal. When a curse was pronounced, the people said, "Amen." When a blessing was pronounced, they also said, "Amen." It was all part of God's law. There were fourteen blessings and fifty-four curses. The blood can wash away these curses.

2. He Eliminated the Curse of the Law of Moses

"Took it out of the way"

"Christ hath redeemed us from the curse of the law, being made a curse for us: for it is written, Cursed is every one that hangeth on a tree" (Galatians 3:13). Some people struggle with this. They ask, "If Jesus came to blot out all curses, how can a Christian still be under a curse?" This is possible because Galatians 3:13 refers to a specific set of curses—those tied to the law of Moses concerning righteousness.

Under that law, sin brought curses because righteousness depended on obeying those laws. Born-again Christians are not under that law because their righteousness is based on faith in the shed blood of Jesus.

Besides this, there are also many sources of curses. For example, the curse God placed on humanity: "In the sweat of thy face shalt thou eat bread, till thou return unto the ground; for out of it wast thou taken: for dust thou art, and unto dust shalt thou return" (Genesis 3:19); curses for breaking God's law, which can be found in the New Testament. Some Old Testament curses are upheld in the New Testament, like honoring your parents.

3. We Become Righteous by Faith

"Nailing it to his cross"
When Jesus was nailed to the cross, He put an end to the law of Moses for righteousness. He nailed the law of Moses concerning righteousness on the cross and brought it to an end, "For Christ is the end of the law for righteousness to every one that believeth" (Romans 10:4). Now we are made righteous by faith, not by the law. "Even the righteousness of God which is by faith of Jesus Christ unto all and upon all them that believe: for there is no difference" (Romans 3:22).

Some people still mix the law of Moses with the law of Christ. They may say women should not wear trousers, or you should worship on a particular day or dress in a particular way or not eat certain foods like pork. "Forbidding to marry, and commanding to abstain from meats, which God hath created to be received with thanksgiving of them which believe and know the truth" (1 Timothy 4:3).

Colossians 2:15
"And having spoiled principalities and powers, he made a shew of them openly, triumphing over them in it."

WHAT HAPPENED ON THE CROSS? continued

4. He Overcame Satanic Powers on Our Behalf

"Spoiled principalities and powers"

MEANING OF PRINCIPALITY

"Principality"
It comes from the word "principal," and it means first in rank, place, or time. It implies a hierarchy. Powers originally meant ability or force. These two words are used in relation to spirits or human beings. For example, Paul says, "Put them in mind to

be subject to principalities and powers, to obey magistrates"—the rulers of the community. So he used the words "principalities and powers" (Titus 3:1).

In a spiritual context Paul said, "We wrestle not against flesh and blood, but against principalities, against powers" (Ephesians 6:12). So it applies to both human rulers and spiritual forces.

MEANING OF POWERS

"Powers"

This means ability, force, because authority must have power behind it. If you're a president, you can't rule without an army or police to enforce your decrees. Demons are part of Satan's army and enforce his will.

Paul reminded them that Jesus destroyed all principalities and powers. Jesus declared that, "All power is given unto me in heaven and in earth" (Matthew 28:18). So no matter what demonic or satanic attack you face, remember: Christ has already destroyed these forces, and in His name, you can overcome them in the mighty name of Jesus.

MEANING OF SPOILED

"Spoiled"

It means to strip off. On the cross the devil was stripped of his power. Jesus used death as a Trojan horse to enter his headquarters.

We Have to Use the Power We Have in Jesus' Name

If I give you a check for a million dollars, even though you didn't earn it, you can go to the bank, use my name, and withdraw the money. The power of withdrawal is in my name, the signature on the check. Blood is the signature of Jesus.

My Encounter with Demons

Personally, I've faced many satanic and demonic attacks, both physically and spiritually. Some time ago I was in Liberia and had a startling experience. I was asleep in my hotel room when suddenly, around 2:00 a.m., I woke up. When the Holy Spirit wakes me, it's always abrupt, and I'm instantly alert—as if I've been awake for hours. This time, I heard someone in my bathroom: the shower was running, the toilet flushed, the tap turned on. A real person seemed to be bathing.

I thought, *Who is that?* I checked the door—it was locked. Then I realized that something was in my bathroom. The Holy Spirit told me, "Don't move. Just pray."

So I stayed in bed, praying and praying until I fell back asleep. The next morning, I found shocking evidence: soap all over the floor, water splashed around, and bubbles. Someone (or something) had clearly bathed there.

The Holy Spirit said, "The spirit wanted to lure you into the bathroom, but you refused. All that was a trap to draw you in." The demon couldn't reach me, but it left physical proof behind. I stayed in that room for four more days. I wasn't running anywhere. In fact, I was angry the spirit had invaded my space, so I declared, "I won't leave till this spirit flees!" For three nights, I battled in prayer. On the third night, I had the victory, and the spirit left.

Why was I so confident? Because I am conscious of the fact that Christ has given us power over all principalities and powers. I stood in faith, knowing I would overcome.

Maybe you're facing nightmares or demonic attacks. Remember that Jesus has given you power over all the enemy's might.

Why Did Jesus Have to Die?

The only way for Jesus to conquer death was to die as a man. When Jesus died, He entered the devil's domain legally, like a spy behind enemy lines, and defeated the devil. He destroyed every principality and power—and set us free. Death became a Trojan horse and gave Jesus access into the devil's kingdom.

Colossians 2:16

"Let no man therefore judge you in meat, or in drink, or in respect of an holyday, or of the new moon, or of the sabbath days."

CONCERNING THE JUDGMENT OF MEN

We should not allow ourselves to be spiritually judged In the following areas:

1. What to Eat or Drink

"In meat, or in drink"
Paul refutes the idea that spirituality is determined by dietary restrictions. Some avoid certain foods for spiritual reasons, like those who avoid pork, claiming it's unclean. Paul reminds us that in Christ, we are free to eat anything as long as it aligns with our conscience. Prayer and the Word sanctify food. "For every creature of God is good, and nothing is to be refused, if it be received with thanksgiving" (1 Timothy 4:4).

2. Holy Days

"In respect of an holyday, or of the sabbath days"
Some argue over which day should be set aside for worship: whether Saturday or Sunday. According to Paul, the specific day isn't what matters; it's the heart of worship that counts.

3. Festivals

"New moon"
We are not required to observe any special days. In the Old Testament, Israel followed a lunar calendar, and their festivals were tied to the phases of the moon. For instance, the Passover, Pentecost (Feast of Weeks), and the Feast of Tabernacles were all significant events marked by the lunar cycle. These festivals were shadows of things to come, pointing to Christ, who is the fulfillment of the law.

Colossians 2:17

"Which are a shadow of things to come; but the body is of Christ."

THE LAW IS A SHADOW; THE REALITY IS CHRIST

"Which are a shadow of things to come; but the body is of Christ"
What is a shadow? Sometimes depending on the angle of the sun, a man's shadow can be cast on the ground before his body comes into view. Shadows give an idea but lack details. The

Old Testament is the shadow of Christ, but Christ is the reality. Following Christ means freedom from the bondage of these laws.

Christ Is the End of the Law
"For Christ is the end of the law for righteousness to every one that believeth" (Romans 10:4). The Old Testament laws, with their 613 commandments, were impossible to keep perfectly. Christ's sacrifice fulfilled the requirements of the law, making His blood the sole basis for our righteousness.

Today, some people still try to enforce Old Testament rules as measures of righteousness, like specific dress codes or dietary restrictions. Paul warns against this. Our righteousness comes through Christ alone, not through external observances.

Colossians 2:18

"Let no man beguile you of your reward in a voluntary humility and worshipping of angels, intruding into those things which he hath not seen, vainly puffed up by his fleshly mind."

DON'T BE DECEIVED AND DEPRIVED OF YOUR SPIRITUAL REWARDS

"Let no man beguile you of your reward"
The reward is righteousness by faith. This can be done through the following:

1. False Humility

"Voluntary humility"
Paul warns against pretending to be humble for the sake of appearances. True humility is a state of the heart and mind. "Let this mind be in you, which was also in Christ Jesus" (Philippians 2:5).

An Example of False Humility
I once spoke with a young woman who appeared deeply spiritual, expressing a desire to know her calling and serve in missions. However, when pressed, she admitted her real concern was

wanting to get married. This was an example of false humility: saying one thing outwardly while harboring a different motive inwardly.

2. Worshipping Angels

"Worshipping of angels"
Some people elevate angels, praying to them or seeking their intervention. This practice is unbiblical. Angels are ministering spirits sent to serve believers (Hebrews 1:14), not beings to be worshipped.

My Angelic Experience
One day, I gave my passport to someone. The passport had all my visas inside, and I was scheduled to travel soon. That night, thieves broke into her car, stole everything, and disappeared with my passport. In the morning, she called me, panicked, saying, "They've stolen your passport!" I responded, "Don't worry; I will pray."

I remembered that angels are ministering spirits sent to serve believers—we are not supposed to serve them (Hebrews 1:14). So I prayed, asking the Lord to send angels to conduct a house-to-house, room-to-room, and pocket-to-pocket search across the whole of Accra until my passport was found.

That same afternoon, around 4 or 5 p.m., the person called me again. "You won't believe what has happened," she said. "Your passport is lying in front of my door, but everything else that was stolen is still missing." I realized that God had answered my prayer. Angels had retrieved my passport and returned it.

This experience reminded me of the correct relationship we should have with angels. They are sent to serve us, not to be worshipped. Jesus said, "Thinkest thou that I cannot now pray to my Father, and he shall presently give me more than twelve legions of angels?" (Matthew 26:53).

We can pray and ask the Lord to release angels to work on our behalf. However, worshipping angels is unbiblical.

Colossians 2:19
"And not holding the Head, from which all the body by joints and bands having nourishment ministered, and knit together, increaseth with the increase of God."

WE SHOULD UPHOLD AND ELEVATE CHRIST ABOVE EVERYTHING

"Not holding the Head"
We should hold or elevate Christ above the laws of Moses. While pastors and leaders play significant roles, the ultimate head of the Church is Christ. Understanding this helps us stay grounded, recognizing that all growth and nourishment in the Church come from Him.

The most important relationship in a believer's life is their connection with Christ and the Holy Spirit. Some Christians are more focused on church activities or even the Bible itself but lack a personal relationship with the Holy Spirit.

You can have three types of relationships as a Christian:

1. A Relationship with the Word – This involves studying and knowing the Bible.
2. A Relationship with the Church – This involves being active in fellowship and ministry.
3. A Relationship with the Holy Spirit – This is the most crucial relationship, as the Holy Spirit is Christ's direct representative on earth.

Without the Holy Spirit, our understanding of the Word and our participation in the church become superficial. Nicodemus is an example of someone who had knowledge of the Scriptures but lacked understanding of spiritual matters. Jesus said to him, "Art thou a master of Israel, and knowest not these things?" (John 3:10).

THE CHURCH IS THE INSTRUMENT CHRIST USES TO MINISTER TO HIS BODY

"from which all the body by joints and bands having nourishment ministered"

The church serves as a vessel through which God supplies blessings to His people. For example, as a pastor, I've introduced church members to opportunities that led to employment.

Many marriages have started with introductions made within the church. Even I met my wife through a church member who was one of my converts. Also, the church community offers encouragement, prayers, and practical assistance.

God has chosen the church as a specific place for blessings, much like oil and gold are found in specific locations. While offenses may occur in the church, Paul reminds us of the importance of staying connected. There are Christians who have been hurt and offended and choose to stay out of fellowship; they forget they don't make the rules—God makes the rules. Be connected and enjoy the blessings.

Colossians 2:20

"Wherefore if ye be dead with Christ from the rudiments of the world, why, as though living in the world, are ye subject to ordinances?"

CHRISTIANS SHOULD BE UNRESPONSIVE TO THE FOLLOWING

1. The World

"Dead with Christ from the rudiments of the world"

"Rudiments" means worldly arrangement or systems. I remember when my father died, he did not respond to his name, our tears, or our cries. He was totally insensitive.

In the same way Christians should not be controlled by worldly systems like cohabitation, debt, the love of money, etc. The Bible encourages us to live within our means and be content with what we have. When Paul said, "I can do all things through

Christ which strengtheneth me," he meant living within your budget (Philippians 4:13).

2. Rules and Traditions

"Ordinances"
"Ordinances" means rules. When we are in Christ, we are no longer bound by the Old Testament arrangement of rules and traditions. For example, dietary laws, such as avoiding pork, were designed to make people righteous under the old covenant. However, under the new covenant, righteousness comes through the blood of Jesus.

Colossians 2:21-22
"(Touch not; taste not; handle not; Which all are to perish with the using;) after the commandments and doctrines of men?"

CHRISTIANS SHOULD BE UNRESPONSIVE TO THE FOLLOWING continued

3. Dietary Laws

"Touch not; taste not; handle not"
Paul taught that believers should not be bound by dietary laws. Under Moses, there were many restrictions on what could or couldn't be eaten, but Paul clarified that those laws were never meant to make people righteous; only the blood of Jesus does that. So now, we're free to eat anything.

For example, growing up, my father refused to eat pork for "spiritual reasons." I followed his example until I became born again and realized I wasn't under those Old Testament restrictions. Once I understood this, I started enjoying pork in every form—kebabs, grilled pork, sausages, you name it. My father's adherence to the old laws had unknowingly limited me.

Years ago, I accidentally ate dog meat. It happened during Christmas at a Filipino friend's gathering. They served kebabs, and after eating, my friend asked if I'd seen his dog. Turns out, the "kebabs" were his dog! I was shocked and almost vomited, but honestly, it was well-prepared. I'm not advocating for eating dog, but Paul's point is clear: Don't let human-made rules restrict you. These laws don't define righteousness.

THESE LAWS WILL PERISH

"Which all are to perish with the using"

Such rules are temporary; they don't last or hold eternal value. What matters is your relationship with Christ. Many early believers mixed Jewish customs with their new faith, but Paul reminds us that in Christ, we're free.

If you've been avoiding certain foods, I pray God releases you from that bondage. As Paul said, food is "sanctified by the word of God and prayer" (1 Timothy 4:5). If you choose not to eat something, that's fine—I don't eat dog, not for spiritual reasons, but simply because I don't want to.

Colossians 2:23

"Which things have indeed a shew of wisdom in will worship, and humility, and neglecting of the body; not in any honour to the satisfying of the flesh."

WHY SOME PEOPLE FOLLOW THESE LAWS

1. To Exhibit Their Wisdom

"Which things have indeed a shew of wisdom"

Some rules appear wise but aren't. For example, worldly wisdom says, "Look out for yourself—it's a dog-eat-dog world!" But Scripture teaches the opposite: "Look not every man on his own things, but every man also on the things of others" (Philippians 2:4).

2. To Exhibit False Humility

"Humility"

Some equate clothing in a particular way or not putting on makeup with holiness. But humility isn't about appearance—it's a mindset: "Let this mind be in you, which was also in Christ Jesus" (Philippians 2:5).

3. They Emphasize the Spiritual at the Cost of the Physical

"and neglecting of the body; not in any honour to the satisfying of the flesh"

Some think ignoring physical needs makes them spiritual. But God cares about all of life—your home, health, even going to the toilet (Deuteronomy 23:12-13 mentions it). Having a mindset that physical things of life are bad and spiritual aspects are good is not biblical.

HOLY VS. UNHOLY—NOT PHYSICAL VS. SPIRITUAL

The Old Testament doesn't split life into "physical" and "spiritual." It categorizes things as clean, unclean, or holy (set apart for God). For example, using money to pay school fees is clean; using money for prostitution is unclean; and using money as Scripture directs (e.g., providing for your family) is holy.

NEW TESTAMENT PRINCIPLE: DO ALL THINGS FOR GOD'S GLORY

"Whether therefore ye eat, or drink, or whatsoever ye do, do all to the glory of God." (1 Corinthians 10:31). "And whatsoever ye do in word or deed, do all in the name of the Lord Jesus" (Colossians 3:17).

"In the name of" means by His authority. If God permits it, it's holy. Don't abandon your job, family, or godly pleasures, thinking it makes you spiritual.

ENJOY GOD'S WORLD RESPONSIBLY

Years ago, I tried ice skating in Dubai. Some might say, "Shouldn't you be praying?" But God made ice for our enjoyment. I went with my family to just relax and have a nice time. That glorifies God.

Explore the world! Travel, try new foods, skate, scuba dive—just ensure everything aligns with God's Word. Life isn't just about prayer and worship; it's about enjoying all God's gifts for His glory.

COLOSSIANS CHAPTER 3

Colossians 3:1-2

"If ye then be risen with Christ, seek those things which are above, where Christ sitteth on the right hand of God. Set your affection on things above, not on things on the earth."

IMPLICATION OF RISING WITH CHRIST

"Risen with Christ"

When you become a Christian, you are supposed to bury your old life: lying, stealing, pride, immorality, etc. And you start new life in Christ Jesus. You begin to live for the glory of God by obeying Him. "Know ye not, that so many of us as were baptized into Jesus Christ were baptized into his death? Therefore we are buried with him by baptism into death: that like as Christ was raised up from the dead by the glory of the Father, even so we also should walk in newness of life" (Romans 6:3-4).

The Symbol of Baptism

Baptism is a powerful symbol of this new life. I remember my first water baptism. A friend of mine baptized me in the sea. We went into the water, I went under, and then came back up. It was a symbolic act. Going under the water represents death: the death of your old self. Coming out of the water represents resurrection: your new life in Christ. "Knowing this, that our old man is crucified with him, that the body of sin might be destroyed, that henceforth we should not serve sin" (Romans 6:6).

The word "destroyed" here means "made idle" or "rendered powerless." When you're born again, your old corrupt spirit and nature is destroyed, and the Holy Spirit comes to live in you. This disables or destroys the body, which is evil and remains the same. This is because your newly created righteous spirit will not cooperate with it.

It's Like Changing the Engine of a Car

I once had a car that kept giving me problems. I decided to change the engine, and when I did, the car started performing like it was brand new. That's what happens when you become born again. God takes out the old engine, your sinful nature, and replaces it with a new one—the Holy Spirit. "Therefore if any man be in Christ, he is a new creature: old things are passed away; behold, all things are become new" (2 Corinthians 5:17).

My Salvation Experience

This is exactly what happened to me when I became born again. My pastor, Bishop Dag Heward-Mills, led me to Christ when I was 19 years old. He came to my house and shared the Gospel with me, and led me in the sinner's prayer. On that day, my old sinful nature died, and a new life in Christ began.

WHAT TO DO AFTER YOU ARE RISEN WITH CHRIST

1. Seek Heavenly and Spiritual Things

"Seek those things which are above"

My Worldly Vision

Before I became born again, my dream was to become a very rich man. I had no desire to preach or be a minister. But when I gave my life to Christ, my priorities changed. I stopped seeking money and started seeking God. Jesus said, "For after all these things do the Gentiles seek. But seek ye first the kingdom of God, and his righteousness; and all these things shall be added unto you" (Matthew 6:32-33). The Gentiles (people of the world) seek after natural, physical things—money, cars, houses, vacations, and so on.

As Christians, our primary focus should be on spiritual things. We should seek the Kingdom of God. This means allowing God to rule over every area of our lives—our decisions, emotions, and actions. We should also seek His righteousness; pursue holiness and strive to live a life that pleases God.

2. Focus Your Mind (Affections) on Heavenly Things

"Set your affection on things above"
The word "affection" here refers to your mind. In other words, focus your mind on spiritual things.

For example, I start every day with prayer and Bible reading. This is my quiet time, where I communicate with God and meditate on His Word. By doing this, I'm setting my mind on things above. Some people only read their Bibles in church or during special occasions. But as born-again Christians, we should be intentional about exposing our minds to spiritual things.

Why I Listen to Only Christian Music
I listen to Gospel music because I believe that words carry spirits. "The words that I speak unto you, they are spirit, and they are life" (John 6:63). That's why I avoid secular music and focus on praise and worship.

I'm also very careful about what I watch. If I'm watching a movie and there's a nude scene, I skip it. I protect my mind because I want to keep it focused on spiritual things.

Colossians 3:3
"For ye are dead, and your life is hid with Christ in God."

WHY YOU MUST SET YOUR MIND (AFFECTION) ON HEAVENLY THINGS (ABOVE)

1. You are Spiritually Dead (Insensitive)

"For ye are dead"
This means to be spiritually dead to sin. When you become born again, you die to your old sinful nature. A dead person is insensitive to the world around them. For example, when my father passed away, I called and touched him but he did not respond. Why? Because he was dead.

In the same way, as Christians, we are spiritually dead to sin. This means we shouldn't be controlled by envy, bitterness, or anger. A dead person can't hold grudges or react to offenses. Paul is reminding us that our old nature is gone, and we are now alive in Christ.

2. Your Real Life, Eternal Life (Zoe), Will Be Manifested When Christ Returns

"Your life is hidden with Christ in God"

The word "life" here is the Greek word *zoe*, which refers to eternal life. This eternal life is hidden from people who don't know God.

Before I became born again, I couldn't understand why people went to church, sang songs, or gave offerings. It all seemed strange to me. The reason is that the life of a Christian was hidden from me because I was spiritually blind and deaf. "But if our gospel be hid, it is hid to them that are lost: in whom the god of this world hath blinded the minds of them which believe not, lest the light of the glorious gospel of Christ, who is the image of God, should shine unto them" (2 Corinthians 4:3-4).

Unbelievers are spiritually blind and deaf. They can't understand the things of God. That's why they criticize pastors and churches. But the day you become born again, the hidden life of a Christian becomes clear to you.

This life will be fully manifested when Jesus returns. That is why we must remain focused on Him.

Colossians 3:4

"When Christ, who is our life, shall appear, then shall ye also appear with him in glory."

THIS LIFE WILL BE FULLY MANIFESTED WHEN CHRIST RETURNS TO THE EARTH

"When Christ, who is our life, shall appear, then shall ye also appear with him in glory."

Right now, as Christians, we may look like fools to the world. In the workplace, for example, people lie, cheat, and manipulate to get ahead, while we strive to live by God's principles. It may seem like we're losing out, but Paul assures us that when Christ returns, our true life or glory will be revealed.

This doesn't mean we can't experience God's blessings now. We do! But the full manifestation of what it means to be a Christian will happen when Christ returns.

THINGS THAT WILL HAPPEN WHEN CHRIST RETURNS

a. Our Bodies Will Change

Paul describes the transformation of our bodies: "It is sown in corruption; it is raised in incorruption. It is sown in dishonour; it is raised in glory. It is sown in weakness; it is raised in power. It is sown a natural body; it is raised a spiritual body" (1 Corinthians 15:42-44).

Our current bodies are weak and subject to death, but when Christ returns, we'll receive glorified bodies that are perfect and eternal.

My Vision of Heaven

I once had a vision of heaven. The people I saw were all in their prime—around 20 to 30 years old, and their bodies glowed with a radiant light. This is how I believe we'll look when Christ returns.

b. We'll Be Made a Quickening Spirit

Paul says, "The first man Adam was made a living soul; the last Adam was made a quickening spirit" (1 Corinthians 15:45).

Adam was a living soul. He was governed by his soul: his mind, emotions, and will. Jesus was made a quickening or living spirit. The Holy Spirit governs His body directly. One day the Spirit of God will govern us directly.

In Ezekiel's vision of the cherubim, he saw them, guided directly by the Spirit, "And they went every one straight forward: whither the spirit was to go, they went; and they turned not when they went" (Ezekiel 1:12). They went where the Spirit went, not where the mind went. This is a picture of how we'll function in our glorified bodies.

c. Our Environment Will Change

John writes, "And I saw a new heaven and a new earth: for the first heaven and the first earth were passed away; and there was no more sea. And I John saw the holy city, new Jerusalem, coming down from God out of heaven" (Revelation 21:1-2).

When Christ returns, we'll live in a brand-new heaven and earth, free from sin, death, and corruption.

Colossians 3:5

"Mortify therefore your members which are upon the earth; fornication, uncleanness, inordinate affection, evil concupiscence, and covetousness, which is idolatry."

HOW SHOULD WE LIVE IN THE LIGHT OF THESE PROMISES?

1. Deaden Your Body

"Mortify therefore your members"

The word "mortify" here means deaden or to become insensitive. In other words, we must not let our bodies respond to sin. Paul lists specific sins that we must resist:

a. *Fornication*

This refers to sexual relations between unmarried people. Adultery, on the other hand, involves a married person having sex with someone other than their spouse. Paul says we must deaden our bodies to these temptations.

b. *Uncleanness*

This refers to impurity. For example watching pornography gives you an impure mind. "And the very God of peace sanctify you wholly; and I pray God your whole spirit and soul and body be preserved blameless unto the coming of our Lord Jesus Christ" (1 Thessalonians 5:23). Our spirit can be corrupted by evil spirits, our soul (mind, will, and emotions) can be corrupted by sin, and our bodies can be corrupted by immoral actions. We must remove all impurity from every part of our being.

c. Inordinate Affection

This refers to unnatural or excessive passions. Paul warns us not to let our bodies respond to these unhealthy desires, like a craving for prostitutes, drugs, or porn.

d. Evil Concupiscence

This means a strong desire for something forbidden. In Greek, there are several words for love: *Agape*: Selfless, Godly love. *Storge*: Love between family members. *Phileo*: Brotherly love. *Eros*: Romantic or sexual love. However, *epithumia* (concupiscence) refers to a depraved, unnatural desire. For example, some people fall in love with animals or engage in other immoral behaviors. This kind of love is outside the normal spectrum and is deeply sinful.

e. Covetousness

This means greed—an insatiable desire for more. "There is one alone, and there is not a second; yea, he hath neither child nor brother: yet is there no end of all his labour; neither is his eye satisfied with riches; neither saith he, For whom do I labour, and bereave my soul of good? This is also vanity, yea, it is a sore travail" (Ecclesiastes 4:8). Covetousness is a never-ending desire for more, and Paul warns us against it.

Colossians 3:6

"For which things' sake the wrath of God cometh on t he children of disobedience."

CONSEQUENCES OF DISOBEDIENCE

"The wrath of God cometh on the children of disobedience"

Anger is an emotion, but wrath is the expression of that emotion. For example, I might be angry with someone but not act on it. However, if I slap them, that's wrath.

Paul warns that disobedience attracts God's wrath. Even as Christians, we can face God's discipline if we persist in sin. "For the wrath of God is revealed from heaven against all ungodliness and unrighteousness of men, who hold the truth in unrighteousness"

(Romans 1:18). This means that even those who know the truth but choose to live in sin will face God's wrath.

Colossians 3:7
"In the which ye also walked some time, when ye lived in them."

A CHRISTIAN MUST DEPART FROM HIS PREVIOUS SINFUL LIFE

Before you knew the Lord, you led a sinful life. The suggestion here is to depart from that lifestyle.

Colossians 3:8
"But now ye also put off all these; anger, wrath, malice, blasphemy, filthy communication out of your mouth."

WE MUST PUT A STOP TO THE FOLLOWING

1. Anger and Wrath

Anger is a negative emotion, while wrath is the physical expression of that anger. Paul says we must control our emotions. A sign of spiritual maturity is the ability to control oneself. "For in many things we offend all. If any man offend not in word, the same is a perfect man, and able also to bridle the whole body" (James 3:2).

It's easier to preach or sing in the choir than to control your anger. Self-control is a mark of a mature Christian. There are Christian people who are verbally or physically abusive when they are angry. Such people must learn self-control with the help of the Holy Spirit.

2. Malice

Malice is the desire to do evil or retaliate when wronged. However, the Bible says, "Be not overcome of evil, but overcome evil with good" (Romans 12:21). Instead of seeking revenge, we must respond with kindness and forgiveness.

3. Blasphemy

This refers to disrespectful or irreverent words against God or others.

4. Filthy Communication

This includes swear words, insults, gossip, and inappropriate language. When Isaiah encountered God, he said, "Woe is me! for I am undone; because I am a man of unclean lips, and I dwell in the midst of a people of unclean lips: for mine eyes have seen the King, the Lord of hosts" (Isaiah 6:5).

Our words matter. A mature Christian controls their tongue and speaks life, not death.

Colossians 3:9

"Lie not one to another, seeing that ye have put off the old man with his deeds."

WE MUST PUT A STOP TO THE FOLLOWING continued

5. Lying

I once knew a Christian man who promised to marry two different women at the same time. He was lying. People lie all the time, from politicians to businessmen to friends to pastors. But a Christian must not lie. You have to put off the old man (the sinful nature). "Knowing this, that our old man is crucified with him, that the body of sin might be destroyed, that henceforth we should not serve sin" (Romans 6:6).

The word "destroyed" means "made idle" or "rendered powerless." When we give our lives to Christ, our old sinful nature is broken, and we receive a new nature through the Holy Spirit.

> ### Colossians 3:10
> *"And have put on the new man, which is renewed in knowledge after the image of him that created him."*

HOW TO PUT ON THE NEW MAN

"Put on the new man"

The new man is our new nature in Christ. "Therefore if any man be in Christ, he is a new creature: old things are passed away; behold, all things are become new" (2 Corinthians 5:17). Becoming a new creature means our habits, desires, and behaviors change to align with God's will.

We put on the new man by renewing our minds with the knowledge of God's Word.

TRANSFORMATION BEGINS WITH THE RENEWING OF OUR MINDS

"Renewed in knowledge"

"And be not conformed to this world: but be ye transformed by the renewing of your mind, that ye may prove what is that good, and acceptable, and perfect, will of God" (Romans 12:2). We renew our minds by reading and meditating on God's Word. Every time we read the Bible, it's like washing our minds of worldly influences and aligning our thoughts with God's truth.

A Disagreement with My Wife

One day, I had a disagreement with my wife. After, I went into my study to pray and read my Bible. As I was reading, I came across a verse that said, "If you have a disagreement with someone and you pray, the Lord will not hear your prayer" (paraphrased). That verse pricked my heart. I realized I needed to renew my mind and align my actions with God's Word. I went back to my wife, apologized, and we reconciled immediately.

How was my mind renewed? It was through reading the Bible. That's why it's so important to read God's Word every day. We constantly pick up "dirt" from the world: wrong ideas, attitudes, and behaviors. Just as Jesus washed Peter's feet because they were dirty from walking, we need to wash our minds with the water of God's Word.

THE STANDARD TO ATTAIN IS THE IMAGE OF GOD

"After the image of him that created him"
As we renew our minds, we begin to look more like Jesus. The goal of reading the Bible isn't just to gain knowledge but also to be transformed into His image. Our character must change, and we must reflect godly attributes.

Colossians 3:11

Where there is neither Greek nor Jew, circumcision nor uncircumcision, Barbarian, Scythian, bond nor free: but Christ is all, and in all."

CHRISTIAN CHARACTER MUST NOT BE NEGATIVELY INFLUENCED BY THE FOLLOWING

Each group mentioned here is symbolic of something.

1. Race: Greek nor Jew
Some people live their lives based on their race or tribe. Their decisions and actions are shaped by cultural or ethnic identity. We are called to look like Jesus, not like someone from our hometown or ethnic group.

2. Education: Greeks
The Greeks were educated and produced scholars like Plato and Aristotle, but Jesus is our standard, not education.

3. Jews: Religion of Works
The Jews followed the law of Moses, which emphasized works and religion but not a transformed life.

He Was Not Born Again
I remember a man dressed as a Catholic priest with a big cross and Bible who sat at the front during a service. As I preached, the Lord told me, "That man is not a priest, and he's not born again." After the service, I asked him, and he admitted he wasn't a priest or a believer. He was just going through the motions.

Rituals without a relationship with Christ are empty. Our goal is to look like Jesus, not to perform religious acts.

4. Circumcision: The Old Covenant

The law of Moses prescribed circumcision as an outward sign of the Jews' covenant with God. In the new covenant, the Holy Spirit in us bears witness that we are the children of God. "The Spirit itself beareth witness with our spirit, that we are the children of God" (Romans 8:16). That is why we must be led by the Spirit of God.

We must not be influenced by the Old Testament requirements of righteousness.

5. Uncircumcision: Unbelievers

This is symbolic of unbelievers because the distinguishing sign between the Jews and the other nations was circumcision. We should not model our lives after unbelievers but after Christ. There are some believers who model their life after sinful, rich men, film and sports stars. Instead of adopting biblical and Christian role models, famous or rich, worldly people become their icons. "Looking unto Jesus the author and finisher of our faith" (Hebrews 12:2).

6. Barbarian: Uneducated

In Paul's time, barbarians were seen as uneducated, while Greeks prided themselves on their knowledge. Education is good, but it shouldn't make us prideful or cause us to lose sight of God. Some people go to Bible school and come out doubting God. Others become so educated that they think they don't need Him. True wisdom comes from knowing Christ. Whether educated or not, we are called to reflect His image.

7. Scythian: Warriors

These were strong warriors. They symbolize successful people according to the standards of the world. We should not model our values, behavior and thinking after worldly "successful people" who live contrary to God's word.

Jesus spoke about a rich man who many will consider a successful person, as a fool. "And he spake a parable unto them, saying, The ground of a certain rich man brought forth plentifully. But God said unto him, Thou fool, this night thy soul shall be required of thee: then whose shall those things be, which thou hast provided?" (Luke 12:16, 20).

Jesus is our ultimate role model.

8. Bond: Social Status

The bonds were the slaves, the lowest in social and economic status. Your social status can influence who you are. We must let the Word determine who we are, not our background, finances, or the depressed community where we live.

9. Free (Economic)

The free were Roman citizens with privilege and money. Some were slave owners. This highlights economic differences. Money can reveal who we are. Some people become arrogant when they gain wealth, while others develop a beggarly mindset when they're poor. In Christ, neither poverty nor riches should define us. We are called to reflect God's character, whether we have little or much. What lesson can we learn from this?

God Is Not a Respecter of Persons

He does not respect your disease, no matter how well-known it is, like cancer, nor your economic situation. Naaman, a powerful military commander, suffered from leprosy. He listened to the advice of his maid and was healed of leprosy (2 Kings 5). Humility and openness to God's Word are key, regardless of our status.

Let's Pray for Healing

Before we pray, let me share a powerful testimony. One day, I was preparing for an all-night service and fell asleep. In my dream, a woman came to me with her son, who had schizophrenia. I prayed for him, and he was healed. Suddenly, my phone rang, waking me up. It was a woman calling from America. She said, "Pastor, my son has schizophrenia. Please pray for him."

I told her, "I was just dreaming about your son. God is going to heal him instantly." I prayed for her son, and when she checked on him, he was completely healed. Later, I met the woman and her son in America. He was now in college, fully healed.

This shows that distance is no barrier to God's healing power. The Bible says, "Is any sick among you? Let him call for the elders of the church; and let them pray over him, anointing him with oil in the name of the Lord: And the prayer of faith shall save the sick, and the Lord shall raise him up" (James 5:14-15).

Let Us Pray for Your Healing if You Are Sick

Father, in Jesus' name, I thank You for anyone reading this book. I pray for those who need healing. I've seen You perform miracles—cancers disappearing, the dead raised, surgeries cancelled. I lift up Your people before You. Have mercy on them. I break the power of sickness. I rebuke schizophrenia and every mental health issue. Let Your peace and joy fill their minds. I curse every satanic force and spirit.

For those believing for a baby, I pray for every complication to be resolved. Tubes, low sperm count, be restored. May you carry your baby in your arms a year from now.

Someone with failing kidneys, receive a brand-new kidney. Creative miracles, happen now. Lord, have mercy. Heal Your people. Let signs and wonders follow them. In Jesus' mighty name. Amen.

Colossians 3:12

"Put on therefore, as the elect of God, holy and beloved, bowels of mercies, kindness, humbleness of mind, meekness, longsuffering."

SPIRITUAL QUALITIES TO DEVELOP

"Put on therefore, as the elect of God"

When you become born again, God has chosen or elected you. Jesus says, "No man can come to me, except the Father which hath sent me draw him" (John 6:44). This means your salvation isn't an accident. God chose you, called you, and drew you to Himself. Because of this, we are to live in a way that honors Him.

Paul uses the phrase "put on," which is like putting on clothes. When you wear clothes, they are visible to everyone. In the same way, the qualities Paul lists should be visible in our lives. He doesn't mention singing, praying, or going to church here. Why? Because those are tools that help us grow in Christ. The real evidence of our faith is the fruit we produce—our character. "For we are his workmanship, created in Christ Jesus unto good works, which God hath before ordained that we should walk in them" (Ephesians 2:10).

SPIRITUAL QUALITIES WE MUST DEVELOP

1. Holiness

"Holy"

Holiness is the first mark of a true believer. "Ye shall know them by their fruits" (Matthew 7:16-20). Holiness is being obedient to the Word and the Spirit of God. Many will be turned away from the gates of heaven because of a lack of holiness.

Jesus said, "Not every one that saith unto me, Lord, Lord, shall enter into the kingdom of heaven; but he that doeth the will of my Father which is in heaven. Many will say to me in that day, Lord, Lord, have we not prophesied in thy name? and in thy name have cast out devils? and in thy name done many wonderful works? And then will I profess unto them, I never knew you: depart from me, ye that work iniquity" (Matthew 7:21-23).

2. Walk in Love

"Beloved"

The word used here is the Greek word *agape*. The God kind of love. The highest form of love—selfless, sacrificial. Paul describes this love: "For when we were yet without strength, in due time Christ died for the ungodly. For scarcely for a righteous man will one die: yet peradventure for a good man some would even dare to die. But God commendeth his love toward us, in that, while we were yet sinners, Christ died for us" (Romans 5:6-8).

Forgiveness Reflects Agape Love

When someone offends you, you forgive them not because they deserve it, but because it's in your nature as a child of God.

The Man Who Owed Me

One day a man owed me a significant amount of money. He had borrowed it when he was sick, and I was happy to help. After some time, I asked him, "Where is my money?" He replied, "God will do it." I thought, *Okay, I'll wait.* A few months later, I saw him again and asked, "Where is my money?" He said, "Pastor, don't you have faith? God will do it." I was starting to get frustrated.

Six months later, I met him again and asked the same question. He gave the same answer: "Pastor, don't you have faith? God will do it." At that moment, God spoke to me and said, "This is an opportunity to show agape love. Just give him the money. Tell him it's a gift. He doesn't deserve it, but that's the nature of agape love."

So I told him, "I've decided to give you this money as a gift. You don't have to pay me back." Do you know what he said? "I told you God would do it!" I felt like slapping him, but that's not what agape love is about.

Agape love isn't transactional. It's not based on what someone deserves. It's about showing kindness and grace, even when the other person doesn't deserve it. Human love is conditional. It says, "I'll love you if you do this for me." But agape love says, "I'll love you no matter what."

3. Empathy

"Bowels of mercies"

The word "bowels" refers to our innermost being—our heart and emotions. This kind of mercy comes from deep within. The best word to describe it is empathy. Empathy is the ability to feel what someone else is feeling because you've been through a similar situation. For example, if you've never struggled with addiction, you might not understand why someone can't stop drinking. If you've never experienced a broken heart, you might say, "Just get over it."

But when you've been through difficult situations, it creates empathy. As a preacher, I've found that God often takes me through challenges to teach me empathy. It's a way of preparing me to minister to others.

The Bible says, "Look not every man on his own things, but every man also on the things of others" (Philippians 2:4). This means we should care about others, not just ourselves. Selfishness is one of the biggest obstacles to empathy.

In marriage, for example, empathy is crucial. Marriage is a union of two people, and each person has dreams and goals. It's not about one person dominating the other but about creating a win-win situation. Empathy helps us understand and support each other.

4. Be Kind

"Kindness"

Kindness is a decision, not just a feeling. It's something we choose to do, even when it's hard. In today's world, kindness is in short supply. People are becoming meaner and more self-centered. Paul warns that, "In the last days, perilous times shall come. For men shall be lovers of their own selves" (2 Timothy 3:1-2).

But as Christians, we are called to be different. We are called to show kindness to everyone: our friends, our enemies, our family, and even strangers.

A Little Act of Kindness Makes a Difference

I remember a classmate of mine who was sick. I hadn't seen him in two years, but I felt led to show him kindness. I called him and said, "I'm sending you some money." It was a small act, but it made a big difference.

Kindness is more than just going to church or singing in the choir. Those are tools, but kindness is the product. It's the evidence of our faith.

David's Kindness to Mephibosheth

One of my favorite stories about kindness is found in 2 Samuel. David asked, "Is there yet any that is left of the house of Saul, that I may show him kindness for Jonathan's sake?" (2 Samuel 9:1).

David and Saul's families were enemies. There had been a long war between them, and David was now in a position of power. But instead of seeking revenge, David chose to show kindness. He found Mephibosheth, Jonathan's son, and restored his inheritance. David said, "I will show him the kindness of God" (2 Samuel 9:3).

This is a powerful example of how we should treat others, even our enemies. God gives us power, money, and influence not to belittle others, but to show kindness.

5. Be Humble

"Humbleness of mind"

The word "humbleness" is also translated as "lowliness of mind." "Let nothing be done through strife or vainglory; but in lowliness of mind let each esteem other better than themselves" (Philippians 2:3). Humility is a mindset, not just an outward appearance. It's about how we think and make decisions.

Paul warns us not to make decisions out of strife. Strife is conflict or competition, and a humble person doesn't act out of anger or retaliation. For example, in marriage, some people withhold love, communication, or intimacy to manipulate their spouse. This is not humility. Humility makes decisions based on God's Word, not emotions.

Even Jesus demonstrated this on the cross. He said, "Father, forgive them; for they know not what they do" (Luke 23:34). He didn't respond to His enemies with strife but with forgiveness.

I pray that you won't make decisions out of strife. Whether it's leaving a church because of a parking issue or holding a grudge against a colleague. Humility seeks peace and follows God's will.

6. Be Meek

"Meekness"

Meekness is closely related to humility. It's not weakness but strength under the control of God's word and will as revealed by the Holy Spirit. "Let this mind be in you, which was also in Christ Jesus: Who, being in the form of God, thought it not robbery to be equal with God: But made himself of no reputation, and took upon him the form of a servant, and was made in the likeness of men: And being found in fashion as a man, he humbled himself, and became obedient unto death, even the death of the cross" (Philippians 2:5-8).

It's not about looking sad or crying in church. It's about having a mindset that's willing to obey God, even when it's difficult.

Jesus demonstrated meekness when He humbled Himself and became obedient to death, even death on the cross (Philippians 2:8). True humility and meekness are shown through obedience to God's Word and the leading of the Holy Spirit. It's about surrendering our will to God's will, even when it's hard.

7. Endurance

"Longsuffering"
Longsuffering means the ability to go through hardship or inconvenience for a long time without complaining. In today's world, where people have short fuses, longsuffering is a rare but powerful quality. It's a sign of the Holy Spirit's work in our lives. Longsuffering is listed as part of the fruit of the Spirit: "But the fruit of the Spirit is love, joy, peace, longsuffering, gentleness, goodness, faith" (Galatians 5:22).

Attending church regularly for decades, even when it's inconvenient or challenging, is a form of longsuffering. Staying committed in marriage, friendships, or business, even when things get tough, demonstrates this quality. Longsuffering is essential for inheriting God's promises. "That ye be not slothful, but followers of them who through faith and patience inherit the promises" (Hebrews 6:12).

Colossians 3:13

"Forbearing one another, and forgiving one another, if any man have a quarrel against any: even as Christ forgave you, so also do ye."

HOW TO RELATE WITH OTHERS

1. Be Tolerant

"Forbearing one another"
Forbearance means tolerating the weaknesses and shortcomings of others. It's about being patient with people, even when they annoy or frustrate us.

The Woman Who Couldn't Take "Nonsense"

I remember speaking to a woman who said, "I've not married because I can't tolerate nonsense." I asked her, "What can't you tolerate?" She replied, "Just this afternoon, I've slapped three people." I was shocked and took a step back, thinking I might be the fourth!

Some people pride themselves on not tolerating nonsense, but that's not the way of Christ. The Bible says, "We then that are strong ought to bear the infirmities of the weak, and not to please ourselves" (Romans 15:1).

What creates intolerance is the urge to please ourselves. We want things our way, but if we want to please God, we'll be more tolerant.

In the workplace, for example, some bosses can't tolerate mistakes. They insult, belittle, and chastise their employees, leaving them broken. But forbearance means helping others grow, not tearing them down. Jesus demonstrated this with His disciples, "Having loved his own which were in the world, he loved them unto the end" (John 13:1). This included Judas, who was stealing money from the group. Jesus knew about it but tolerated it, hoping Judas would change.

I'm not saying we should tolerate evil, but within the bounds of Scripture, we must be patient with others. Be patient with your husband as he grows. Be tolerant with your pastor as he learns. Be understanding with your father, who's also figuring things out.

2. Forgive

"Forgiving one another"

Forgiveness is Christlike. That's why they say forgiveness is divine. Jesus says, "Therefore if thou bring thy gift to the altar, and there rememberest that thy brother hath ought against thee; leave there thy gift before the altar, and go thy way; first be reconciled to thy brother, and then come and offer thy gift" (Matthew 5:23-24).

If someone has hurt you—whether it's a friend who betrayed you, a boss who wronged you, or a brother who refused to help you—forgive them. Don't hold onto bitterness. Jesus forgave us, and we must do the same. Forgiveness is a powerful sign that we are children of God.

Colossians 3:14

"And above all these things put on charity, which is the bond of perfectness."

HOW TO RELATE WITH OTHERS continued

3. Put on love

"Put on charity"

Most of the time, our love is transactional: "If you're nice to me, I'll love you. If you give to me, I'll love you." But agape love is not transactional. It's selfless and unconditional. "But God commendeth his love toward us, in that, while we were yet sinners, Christ died for us" (Romans 5:8). The word "commendeth" means God initiated His love. He didn't wait for us to deserve it.

Sometimes people say, "The younger person should apologize to the elder, or the offender must apologize to the offended." But in the Bible, it's different. Christ, the more powerful and elder One, initiated the love. That's why Paul says we should initiate love, even if we're older, richer, or more powerful. Have you had a cold war with your spouse before? Being the one who breaks the war and tries to reconcile, regardless of who is wrong, is exhibiting agape love.

Abraham Demonstrated This Kind of Love Towards Lot

Abraham was older and richer than Lot, but when there was strife, he took the initiative to resolve it. Abraham said to Lot, "Let there be no strife, I pray thee, between me and thee…for we be brethren. Is not the whole land before thee? separate thyself, I pray thee, from me: if thou wilt take the left hand, then I will go to the right; or if thou depart to the right hand, then I will go to the left" (Genesis 13:8-9).

THE POWER OF LOVE

1. Love Bonds People Together

"The bond of perfectness"

Paul says love is the "bond of perfectness." It's the glue that holds relationships together. Love keeps marriages, families, friendships, and churches united. When we lack love, relationships fall apart.

2. Love Is a Sign of Maturity

Paul calls love the "bond of perfectness," which means it's a sign of maturity. Demonstrating agape love shows that we are spiritually mature.

Sometimes people think maturity is about praying for hours, quoting Greek words, or having deep spiritual revelations. But the Bible says maturity is about love. Paul says, "We then that are strong ought to bear the infirmities of the weak, and not to please ourselves" (Romans 15:1).

If there's a quarrel in your home, the mature person initiates reconciliation. Don't wait for the other person to apologize. Remember, God commended His love toward us. He initiated it. Grace isn't for the one who's right; it's for the humble.

Colossians 3:15

"And let the peace of God rule in your hearts, to the which also ye are called in one body; and be ye thankful."

THE PEACE OF GOD SHOULD GUIDE OUR DECISIONS

"let the peace of God rule in your hearts"

The Holy Spirit lives in us, and He is also called the Spirit of peace. We must allow the peace of God to do the following.

1. Lead Us (Rule)

"Let the peace of God rule"

The word "rule" here is like an umpire in a tennis match. The umpire moderates the game, determines what's right or wrong, and guides the match. Similarly, the peace of God should act as our umpire, guiding our decisions and actions.

Just as you can identify a tree by its fruit, you can identify the presence of God by His fruit. When you have peace in your heart about something, it's a sign that God is with you. That's why it's called the fruit of the Spirit. It shows that the Holy Spirit is at work in your life.

One of the fruits of the Spirit is peace. "But the fruit of the Spirit is love, joy, peace, longsuffering, gentleness, goodness, faith, meekness, temperance" (Galatians 5:22-23). When the Holy Spirit is present in a situation or in someone's life, all of this, including peace, will be present. Remember, it's the fruit, singular, of the Spirit.

How I Detected a Mouse in My House

One day I bought a loaf of bread and left it in the kitchen. When I woke up the next morning, I saw bite marks on the bread. I didn't see the mouse, but the bite marks told me a mouse was there. In the same way, even if we can't see the Holy Spirit, His presence is revealed through the fruit of peace.

For example, if you have a quarrel with your spouse or a misunderstanding with your brother, ask yourself, *Do I have peace within myself?* If the answer is no, remember that the Holy Spirit has ruled in the situation.

The Man Who Kept Receipts of His Gifts to His Girlfriend

I know someone who kept receipts for every gift he bought his girlfriend during their relationship—even for bottles of water and biscuits. When they broke up, he presented her with all the receipts and demanded repayment. That decision didn't bring peace; it only increased animosity.

2. Peace Brings Unity

"Ye are called in one body"

You have been called to be a part of the body of Christ (Church). This understanding helps us maintain good relationships. The Bible says, "And he gave some, apostles; and some, prophets; and some, evangelists; and some, pastors and teachers; For the perfecting of the saints, for the work of the ministry, for the edifying of the body of Christ" (Ephesians 4:11-12).

As part of the body of Christ, we are called to build up the church, not tear it down. If my hand accidentally hits my face, my face doesn't decide to leave my body. It stays because it's part of the same body. In the same way, when we feel hurt or unappreciated in church, we shouldn't let anger or disappointment drive us away.

There's no perfect church. If you find one, don't join it—because the moment you do, it will stop being perfect! We need tolerance and forbearance to maintain good relationships within the body of Christ.

3. Be Thankful

"Be ye thankful"

Gratitude is key to maintaining good relationships. Everyone has good and bad qualities. If we focus on the negative, we become critical and bitter. But if we focus on the positive, we find reasons to be thankful. "Be careful for nothing; but in every thing by prayer and supplication with thanksgiving let your requests be made known unto God" (Philippians 4:6). Even when someone has hurt us, we can find something to be thankful for.

For example, you might say, "My mother-in-law was so wicked to me. How can I be thankful?" But if you look closely, you might realize that she helped raise your spouse, who is now a blessing to you. Even if someone has flaws, there's always something good to focus on. "Finally, brethren, whatsoever things are true, whatsoever things are honest, whatsoever things are just, whatsoever things are pure, whatsoever things are lovely, whatsoever things are of good report; if there be any virtue, and if there be any praise, think on these things" (Philippians 4:8).

When we focus on the good in others, it helps us maintain healthy relationships. Be thankful for your pastor, who sacrifices to lead the church. Be thankful for your parents, who worked hard to raise you. Be thankful for your friends, who support you. Gratitude strengthens relationships and helps us see the best in people.

Colossians 3:16
*"Let the word of Christ dwell in you
richly in all wisdom; teaching and admonishing one another
in psalms and hymns and spiritual songs, singing with grace
in your hearts to the Lord."*

HOW TO LET THE WORD OF GOD DWELL IN YOU RICHLY

1. Teaching

"Let the word of Christ dwell in you richly in all wisdom; teaching"
We must expose ourselves to teaching and also teach others. When you are taught, you grow in understanding. And when you teach others, your own understanding deepens. It's like a student in a classroom. You attend class, learn the material, and when you explain it to your classmates, you grasp it even more.

"For Ezra had prepared his heart to seek the law of the Lord, and to do it, and to teach in Israel statutes and judgments" (Ezra 7:10). The best teachers are those who practice what they preach. Your words can never carry more weight than your experience. Why? Because when someone speaks from experience, they become a credible witness. The Bible calls us to be witnesses, not reporters. A reporter shares what they've heard, but a witness shares what they've experienced.

"Whosoever therefore shall break one of these least commandments, and shall teach men so, he shall be called the least in the kingdom of heaven: but whosoever shall do and teach them, the same shall be called great in the kingdom of heaven" (Matthew 5:19). The greatest teachers are those who live by God's Word. When you live by it, you become a credible witness. Experience always outweighs theory.

2. Warning

"Admonish one another"
To admonish means to warn. The Bible frequently warns us about impending danger, God's judgment, and the consequences

of sin. These warnings are crucial. For example, Proverbs says, "A little sleep, a little slumber, a little folding of the hands to sleep: So shall thy poverty come as one that travelleth, and thy want as an armed man" (Proverbs 6:10-11). This is a clear warning that laziness leads to poverty.

Warning to Those Who Think They Are Standing
There is a warning in the Bible to those who think they stand firm to be careful lest they fall. "Wherefore let him that thinketh he standeth take heed lest he fall" (1 Corinthians 10:12). Paul talks about people who have had spiritual experiences—they've been born again, they know the power of God, they've experienced the Holy Spirit—yet they live carelessly. He uses Israel as an example.

They were God's children, rescued from Egypt and led toward Canaan, just as we are rescued from the world and led toward heaven. Yet, along the way, they lived carelessly. "Now all these things happened unto them for examples: and they are written for our admonition, upon whom the ends of the world are come" (1 Corinthians 10:11).

3. Music

"Psalms and hymns and spiritual songs"
The word "psalms" refers to the Word of God put into music. The Bible mentions various instruments: trumpets, flutes, harps, and more that accompany these songs. Psalms are a powerful way to let God's Word dwell in us richly. The words set to music are easy to remember.

Why We Should Not Listen to Worldly Songs
It's important to listen to worship songs, Gospel songs, and Christian music rather than worldly songs. Why? Because words carry a spirit behind them. "The words that I speak unto you, they are spirit, and they are life" (John 6:63). There's a spirit behind words—it's not just the melody or the lyrics. This is why some people become violent after listening to certain types of music. The music plants seeds in their minds, and spirits take control.

The Story of David and Saul
"And it came to pass, when the evil spirit from God was upon Saul, that David took a harp, and played with his hand: so Saul was refreshed, and was well, and the evil spirit departed from him" (1 Samuel 16:23). When David played godly music, it drove out the evil spirit. I've noticed something personally. When you're sick and you listen to Gospel music, it ministers healing to your body. It brings hope, peace, and relaxation. It ushers in the presence of God. This is why we must surround ourselves with Christian music.

Hymns are songs of praise that glorify God. Spiritual songs, on the other hand, are songs that focus on a particular person—in this case, God Himself.

4. Singing

"Singing with grace"
Grace, in this context, means joy. We have to sing with a joyful heart. "God loveth a cheerful giver" (2 Corinthians 9:7). Even when we offer a song to God, let it be given out of love and joy. Singing with grace means worshipping with a heart full of gratitude and delight in the Lord.

5. Sing with Sincerity

"In your hearts to the Lord"
When you sing from the heart, it means your heart is overflowing. Your mouth is the overflow valve of your soul. "A good man out of the good treasure of his heart bringeth forth that which is good; for out of the abundance of the heart his mouth speaketh" (Luke 6:45). Singing from the heart is an expression of what's within us.

"For the LORD seeth not as man seeth; for man looketh on the outward appearance, but the LORD looketh on the heart" (1 Samuel 16:7). When we sing from the heart, God pays attention to our worship.

Sadly, many Christians don't take the time to learn songs. Unbelievers, on the other hand, memorize entire songs and raps. Some Christians can't even sing one Christian song fully; they just hum along. But when you know the words of a song, it gives more meaning to your worship and helps you sing from the heart.

Colossians 3:17

"And whatsoever ye do in word or deed, do all in the name of the Lord Jesus, giving thanks to God and the Father by him."

MOTIVATION FOR EVERYTHING WE SAY OR DO

"Whatsoever ye do in word or deed"

Our words must be backed by the authority of Jesus, and our actions must align with His will. But what does it mean to do something "in the name of Jesus"? Let's break it down.

WHAT IT MEANS TO ACT IN THE NAME OF JESUS

1. You Have His Authority

For example, if I send you somewhere in my name to collect $100, you are coming with my authority. I have given you permission to act on my behalf. Similarly, when we speak or act in the name of Jesus, it means He has given us permission to do so. This permission comes through the Bible and the guidance of the Holy Spirit.

We must not say or do anything that contradicts the Bible. For instance, the Bible says, "Honour thy father and thy mother: that thy days may be long upon the land which the LORD thy God giveth thee" (Exodus 20:12). If you choose to insult or dishonor your parents, you are not acting in the name of Jesus because His Word does not permit such behavior.

2. You Are His Representative

If I go somewhere and say, "I come in the name of the President," it means I am representing the President, not myself. I am not expressing my own opinions or desires; I am conveying the President's will. Similarly, when we act in the name of Jesus, we are representing God. We do not share our own views or act according to our own will. We represent His.

For example, God commands us to forgive our enemies. If I have an enemy and I choose to curse or physically harm them,

Jesus says, "Love your enemies, bless them that curse you, do good to them that hate you, and pray for them which despitefully use you, and persecute you" (Matthew 5:44). As His representative, I am called to love and do good, even to those who hurt me.

Resolving Conflicts As God's Representative
The Bible also teaches that conflicts should be resolved quickly. "Be ye angry, and sin not: let not the sun go down upon your wrath" (Ephesians 4:26). This means we have up to sunset, 24 hours, to resolve any quarrel or problem. As God's representatives, if we hold a grudge beyond this time, we are not acting in His name. Even if the other person refuses to reconcile, we must do our part to seek peace. This is what it means to truly represent God.

HOW TO GIVE THANKS

1. Thanksgiving Must Be Directed to God

"Giving thanks to God and the Father by him"
Thanksgiving must always be directed to God alone. Why? Because everything we have and enjoy comes from Him.

When I wake up in the morning, I start by thanking God for the gift of life, for the ability to walk, and for the seemingly small things we often take for granted. As we grow older, we realize that even the simplest blessings like walking, eating, or having friends are not to be taken lightly. We must thank God for everything: for sleep, for food, for relationships, and for every good thing in our lives.

Thanksgiving is not just an occasional act; it is a lifestyle. We must continually direct our gratitude to God, for He alone is the source of all our blessings. Let us cultivate a heart of thanksgiving, acknowledging Him in all we do.

2. Give Thanks in the Name of Jesus

The Bible instructs us to give thanks in the name of Jesus. This is divine protocol. When we give thanks, we do it through Jesus. For example, I might pray, "Lord, I bless You, in Jesus' name. I thank You for my parents, my wife, my job, my health, and the peace You've given me. I thank You and bless You, in Jesus' name." Why? Because the name of Jesus is holy and sanctified. It is the name God recognizes. No other name carries the same authority.

A Name Grants Access

To gain access to powerful people, you often need to drop a name. You might say, "Your friend sent me," and suddenly, doors open. It's the same with Jesus. His name is powerful. "Wherefore God also hath highly exalted him, and given him a name which is above every name: That at the name of Jesus every knee should bow, of things in heaven, and things in earth, and things under the earth" (Philippians 2:9-10). His name has authority in heaven, on earth, and even under the earth. So let's give thanks to God in the name of Jesus.

Colossians 3:18

"Wives, submit yourselves unto your own husbands, as it is fit in the Lord."

MARITAL RELATIONSHIPS

1. Wives Should Submit to Their Husbands

"Wives, submit yourselves to your own husbands"

a. *Submission*

This submission is not about inferiority but about recognizing God-ordained authority. The husband has authority over the wife, but this authority is not self-appointed; it is given by God. The verse emphasizes that this submission is "fit in the Lord," meaning it is proper and aligned with God's will.

b. *This Authority Is Conditional*

The husband must be subject to Christ to have this authority. It is a chain of authority. The Bible explains the chain of authority: "But I would have you know, that the head of every man is Christ; and the head of the woman is the man; and the head of Christ is God" (1 Corinthians 11:3). Authority flows from God to Christ, from Christ to the man, and from the man to the woman. This structure ensures order and harmony.

The Husband Must Be Under God's Authority
Some people argue that this verse is unfair, fearing that husbands might misuse their authority. However, the context is crucial. The husband's authority is valid only if he is under the authority of Christ. If a husband is not submitted to God, he cannot rightly expect his wife to submit to him. Authority is conditional; it requires being under authority.

A Centurion Explains This Principle
"For I also am a man set under authority, having under me soldiers, and I say unto one, Go, and he goeth; and to another, Come, and he cometh; and to my servant, Do this, and he doeth it" (Luke 7:8). The centurion had authority because he himself was under authority. Similarly, a husband must be under God's authority to have the right to have authority; otherwise he can abuse his authority.

The tool God gives husbands to lead is not force but love. When a husband loves his wife as Christ loves the church, submission becomes natural. Even animals respond to love and care. Love fosters trust and respect, making authority a blessing rather than a burden.

Colossians 3:19

"Husbands, love your wives, and be not bitter against them."

MARITAL RELATIONSHIPS continued

2. Husbands Should Love Their Wives

"Husbands, love your wives"
The Greek word used here for love is *agape*, which refers to unconditional, sacrificial love.

Taking the Initiative in Love
"But God commendeth his love toward us, in that, while we were yet sinners, Christ died for us" (Romans 5:8). "Commend"

here originally means to take the initiative. God took the initiative to love us while we were still sinners. He didn't wait for us to become perfect or deserving. This is the model for husbands. Agape love means taking the initiative to love your wife, even when she is wrong or when there is conflict.

The role as the head of the household is not conditional on your wife's behavior. You are called to lead with love, regardless of who is right or wrong. When there is a misunderstanding, don't play the blame game or wait for your wife to apologize first. Take the initiative to restore peace. Tell yourself, *The buck stops with me.* It doesn't matter who is at fault; your responsibility is to lead with love and maintain harmony in your home.

3. Husbands Should Not Be Bitter

"Be not bitter against them"

There's a significant difference between unforgiveness and bitterness. Unforgiveness is when you hold onto hurt, but bitterness is when that hurt lingers for a long time and begins to destroy you and your relationships. Bitterness doesn't just affect you—it spreads and damages other connections in your life. "Looking diligently lest any man fail of the grace of God; lest any root of bitterness springing up trouble you, and thereby many be defiled" (Hebrews 12:15).

Bitterness Troubles Relationships

In marriages, for example, bitterness can become so intense that spouses can't stand to be in the same house. They look for every excuse to stay away—work trips, social outings, anything to avoid being home. Bitterness doesn't just trouble you; it defiles many others. It can affect your relationships with in-laws, siblings, friends, and even your children. It spreads like a poison.

Husbands must ensure that bitterness doesn't take root in their homes. If there's a problem, address it. If there's an issue, bring it up. Even if your wife doesn't want to talk about it, take the initiative. Be the one to steer the conversation and root out bitterness. Don't let it fester and destroy your family.

Colossians 3:20
"Children, obey your parents in all things:
for this is well pleasing unto the Lord."

INSTRUCTIONS FOR CHILDREN

1. Obey Parents

"Children, obey your parents in all things"
It's important to read this alongside Ephesians 6:1, which adds a crucial detail: "Children, obey your parents in the Lord: for this is right." The phrase "in the Lord" means that children should obey their parents as long as their instructions align with God's Word and the Holy Spirit. If a parent tells a child to do something contrary to Scripture, the child is not obligated to obey.

For example, I've seen cases where parents encourage their children to pursue relationships with already married people. In such situations, the child must not obey because it goes against God's Word. Obedience to parents is important, but it must always be subject to the authority of God. Without this check, human authority can easily be abused. God knows the hearts of men. That is why He places His Word as the ultimate standard.

2. Obedience to Parents Pleases God

"For this is well pleasing unto the Lord"
Many children think that pleasing God only involves going to church or praying, but obedience to parents is also a practical way to honor Him. When you please God, the heavens open over your life. This happened when Jesus pleased the father: "Now when all the people were baptized, it came to pass, that Jesus also being baptized, and praying, the heaven was opened, And the Holy Ghost descended in a bodily shape like a dove upon him, and a voice came from heaven, which said, Thou art my beloved Son; in thee I am well pleased" (Luke 3:21-22). When God is pleased, the heavens open, and blessings flow.

The Bible says, "The LORD shall open unto thee his good treasure, the heaven to give the rain unto thy land in his season, and to bless all the work of thine hand: and thou shalt lend unto many nations, and thou shalt not borrow" (Deuteronomy 28:12). When the heavens open, the work of your hands is blessed. Whether you're studying, working, cooking, or building relationships, everything you do prospers. You become a lender, not a borrower, living a debt-free life. This is the blessing that comes from obeying your parents and pleasing God.

Colossians 3:21

"Fathers, provoke not your children to anger, lest they be discouraged."

FATHERS AND THEIR RELATIONSHIP WITH THEIR CHILDREN

1. Don't Provoke (Stir) Children

"Provoke not your children to anger"

Fathers must be careful not to stir up their children to anger. This can happen when fathers are unreasonable, hypocrites, wicked, shirk their responsibilities, or abuse their spouses.

This can stir up rebellion in children. Jezebel stirred up her husband, Ahab, to do evil. She gave him wrong advice, leading him further into sin. Fathers must avoid doing the same. Don't encourage your children to engage in immoral behavior, such as premarital relationships or dishonesty. Don't mock their faith or discourage them from pursuing God.

Some parents laugh at their children for going to church, reading the Bible, or praying, saying things like, "Are you one of those religious people?" This kind of attitude stirs up negativity and pushes children away from God. Don't be that kind of parent.

2. Encourage Your Children

"Lest they be discouraged"

Instead of discouraging your children, encourage them. As a father of four, I've learned that children don't just need financial support; they need emotional and spiritual encouragement. A little encouragement can go a long way. When your child is struggling academically, talk to them. When they fall, lift them up. Affirm them with words and actions. Your encouragement gives them the energy to keep going.

Encourage your children, your wife, and everyone in your household. Don't try to control or weaken them; instead, help them become the best versions of themselves.

Colossians 3:22

"Servants, obey in all things your masters according to the flesh; not with eyeservice, as menpleasers; but in singleness of heart, fearing God."

DEVELOP GOOD WORK ETHIC

In Paul's time, there were slaves and masters. Today, we have employees and employers. This passage isn't endorsing slavery but rather teaching work ethics. Paul's personal stance on slavery is clear in his letter to Philemon, where he tells Philemon to treat his slave, Onesimus, as a brother, not as property. Here, however, Paul focuses on how we should conduct ourselves in work relationships. Whether you work in a computer firm, a grocery store, a hospital, or any other place, these principles apply.

1. Obey Your Master or Employers

"Obey in all things your masters according to the flesh"

When you're working, it's important to obey your employer. Some people act as if they work for themselves, ignoring their employer's instructions. This is wrong.

Follow the Directives of Your Employer

I once told a group of workers, "You don't work for yourselves; you work for me. Do what I want you to do." Always remember, you're working for someone else, so follow their directives. If you do your own thing, no matter how hard you work, you may not be appreciated because it's not what your employer wants.

2. Work without Supervision (Eye Service)

"Not with eyeservice"

Eye service means working only when someone is watching, like a man-pleaser. Some people only work hard when their boss is around, but as soon as the boss leaves, they slack off. This is not the right attitude.

Ants As an Example of Good Work Ethic

"Go to the ant, thou sluggard; consider her ways, and be wise: Which having no guide, overseer, or ruler, Provideth her meat in the summer, and gathereth her food in the harvest" (Proverbs 6:6-8). Ants work diligently without supervision. They are self-driven.

In our workplaces, we should be like ants—self-motivated and proactive. Don't wait for someone to tell you what to do. Take the initiative, deliver results, and do the right thing whether someone is watching or not. This is the mark of a good work ethic.

3. Don't Be a Man-Pleaser

"As menpleasers"

Being a man-pleaser means doing things just to gain favor or approval from others. This can lead to compromising your integrity and neglecting the development of your skills. The Bible says, "When a man's ways please the LORD, he maketh even his enemies to be at peace with him" (Proverbs 16:7). Focus on pleasing God, not people.

In the workplace, there's often office politics. While politics might yield short-term gains, it doesn't last. In the long run, your character, skills, and work ethic will speak louder than any political maneuvering. Stay away from office politics. Just do your job well, and let your work speak for itself.

4. Be Sincere

"In singleness of heart"

Be genuine in your actions and words. Don't be fake or insincere. Let your work reflect honesty and integrity.

5. Fear God

"Fearing God"
Fearing God is the foundation of a good work ethic. The Bible says, "Having therefore these promises, dearly beloved, let us cleanse ourselves from all filthiness of the flesh and spirit, perfecting holiness in the fear of God" (2 Corinthians 7:1). When you fear God, you'll do the right thing because you know He's watching.

The Man Who Blamed the Devil for His Wrong
I once knew someone who was entrusted with managing a transport business and rental properties while his boss was abroad. When the boss returned, all the money was gone. When I asked why he spent the money, he blamed the devil. But even if the devil tempted him, why did he give in? The real issue was a lack of fear of God. When you fear God, you won't steal, lie, or act dishonestly. You'll do what's right because you know God is your ultimate judge.

Joseph Is a Great Example
When Potiphar's wife tried to seduce Joseph, he refused, saying, "How then can I do this great wickedness, and sin against God?" (Genesis 39:9). Joseph feared God, and that kept him from wrongdoing. If you fear God, you'll avoid dishonesty, laziness, and unethical behavior at work.

Colossians 3:23

"And whatsoever ye do, do it heartily, as to the Lord, and not unto men."

DEVELOP GOOD WORK ETHIC continued

6. Work from Your Heart

"Do it heartily"
To work "heartily" means working with enthusiasm and dedication. Jesus says, "A good man out of the good treasure of his heart bringeth forth that which is good" (Luke 6:45). When you

work from the heart, you bring forth good results. There's zeal, energy, and passion in what you do. Don't work as if you're forced to; work as if it's your own. Treat your job with the same care and commitment as if it were your business.

7. Your Motivation Should Be the Lord

"As to the Lord, and not unto men"
Your motivation matters. While money is important, it shouldn't be your primary motivation. Serve God first. Let your work be an act of worship to Him. When your motivation is aligned with God's will, you'll find greater fulfillment and purpose in your work.

Colossians 3:24

"Knowing that of the Lord ye shall receive the reward of the inheritance: for ye serve the Lord Christ."

GOD WILL REWARD YOU IF YOU WORK WELL

1. God Is Your Rewarder

"Knowing that of the Lord ye shall receive the reward"
Sometimes we think our rewards come only from our employers, but that's not true. God sees your work, and He will reward you. The Israelites worked for the Egyptians for 430 years without pay, but when they left Egypt, God caused the Egyptians to give them gold, silver, and clothing (Exodus 12:35-36).

God rewards those who work diligently and faithfully. "For God is not unrighteous to forget your work and labour of love, which ye have shewed toward his name" (Hebrews 6:10). God remembers your efforts. Even if your employer doesn't appreciate you, God will reward you in His time.

Colossians 3:25
"But he that doeth wrong shall receive for the wrong which he hath done: and there is no respect of persons."

GOD PUNISHES WRONG DOING

1. God Punishes the Unjust

"But he that doeth wrong shall receive for the wrong"

The word "wrong" means unjust. We often forget that God is not only a rewarder but also a judge. "And as it is appointed unto men once to die, but after this the judgment" (Hebrews 9:27). "But ye are come unto mount Sion, and unto the city of the living God, the heavenly Jerusalem, and to an innumerable company of angels, To the general assembly and church of the firstborn, which are written in heaven, and to God the Judge of all" (Hebrews 12:22-23). God is the ultimate Judge, and judges don't just reward—they also punish.

We must remember that God watches us as we work for others. If we're lazy, dishonest, late, or causing problems, we're not just accountable to our employers but to God Himself. He sees everything, and He will judge our actions. This should motivate us to work with integrity, diligence, and a heart that fears God.

COLOSSIANS CHAPTER 4

Colossians 4:1
"Masters, give unto your servants that which is just and equal, knowing that ye also have a Master in heaven."

EMPLOYMENT RELATIONS

1. Fairness

"Give unto your servants that which is just and equal"
The word "just" or "righteous" means doing the right thing. Employers must be righteous in their dealings with their employees. Paul is clear: employers shouldn't cheat employees. Employers should pay people what they deserve, no more, no less. This is practical wisdom from God's Word.

2. Accountability

"Knowing that ye also have a Master in heaven"
Paul gives a powerful reason for treating others justly. Masters or employers are ultimately accountable to the Lord. A case in point is the story of Laban and Jacob. Laban was a wicked employee and God rebuked him. Jacob said, "Thus have I been twenty years in thy house; I served thee fourteen years for thy two daughters, and six years for thy cattle: and thou hast changed my wages ten times. Except the God of my father, the God of Abraham, and the fear of Isaac, had been with me, surely thou hadst sent me away now empty. God hath seen mine affliction and the labour of my hands, and rebuked thee yesternight" (Genesis 31:41-42).

Jesus said, "For with what judgment ye judge, ye shall be judged: and with what measure ye mete, it shall be measured to you again" (Matthew 7:2). This means the standard we use for others will be applied to us. When we're conscious of God's presence, it helps regulate our behavior. It's like driving carefully when you know the police are watching. Similarly, knowing God is watching helps us do the right thing.

Colossians 4:2

"Continue in prayer, and watch in the same with thanksgiving."

TWO THINGS YOU MUST CONTINUE TO DO

1. Continue Praying

"Continue in prayer"

Sometimes we pray for a season and then stop. But prayer should be a daily habit. By God's grace, I've prayed every day for years—not because I'm a pastor, but because I learned the importance of daily prayer when I became born again.

Jesus Admonishes Us to Pray Daily

"After this manner therefore pray ye: Our Father which art in heaven, Hallowed be thy name. Thy kingdom come. Thy will be done in earth, as it is in heaven. Give us this day our daily bread" (Matthew 6:9-11). Notice He said "daily bread," not monthly bread. We must pray for our daily needs—food, clothing, shelter, and finances. I pray that God will provide for you daily.

I've observed that the richest people in the world generate income daily. While you sleep, someone in Tokyo is buying their software, and when Tokyo sleeps, someone in Ghana is making a purchase. It's a continuous cycle. I pray that God will bless you with wisdom to generate daily income, whether through investments, business, or other means.

Pray Because the Devil Never Sleeps

You might go on holiday, but the devil is always working. Peter warns, "Be sober, be vigilant; because your adversary the devil, as a roaring lion, walketh about, seeking whom he may devour" (1 Peter 5:8). The devil is always looking for someone to destroy.

"Finally, my brethren, be strong in the Lord, and in the power of his might. Put on the whole armour of God, that ye may be able to stand against the wiles of the devil. For we wrestle not against flesh and blood, but against principalities, against powers, against the rulers of the darkness of this world, against spiritual wickedness in high places" (Ephesians 6:10-12).

Why I Pray Before Going to Bed Every Day
I remember an experience some time ago. Before I went to bed, I prayed, as the Bible instructs us to pray always. In the middle of the night, something extraordinary happened. While I was asleep, it felt as though my eyes were open, and I could see my room and even outside. It was as if I was both asleep and awake at the same time. This reminds me of Song of Solomon 5:2, which says, "I sleep, but my heart waketh" (Song of Solomon 5:2).

I saw a man with wings flying toward my house from a distance of about two kilometers. In the realm of the spirit, distance doesn't limit vision. As he drew closer, he passed through my bedroom walls and windows, landing right in front of my bed. The moment he landed, I woke up physically and commanded, "Get out in Jesus' name!"

I cast out that evil spirit. Even in the middle of the night, I had to wake up and pray because God had shown me something. You may not see such things, but it doesn't matter. Just pray.

2. Continue Giving Thanks

"With thanksgiving"
Paul continues by emphasizing the importance of thanksgiving. "In every thing give thanks: for this is the will of God in Christ Jesus concerning you" (1 Thessalonians 5:18). This is a challenging Scripture because it calls us to give thanks in everything—both good times and bad.

It's easy to thank God when things are going well, like when you've made a million dollars or passed an exam. But it's much harder to give thanks when you've lost your job, had an accident, or received heartbreaking news. For example, imagine being in a five-year relationship, only to receive a WhatsApp message saying, "Sharon, it's over." Just two words, and years of investment are gone. How do you give thanks in such a situation?

Why We Must Give Thanks
The reason we must give thanks isn't because we feel good, but because of what thanksgiving does. Paul explains, "Quench not the Spirit" (1 Thessalonians 5:19). Thanksgiving releases the Holy Spirit and invites God's presence into our lives. In difficult situations, we need God's influence more than ever.

Focus on the Positives

One way to do this is by focusing on the positives in every situation. For example, if you lose your job it may give you more time with your family. In every bad situation, there are good aspects. Some people are unhappy in their marriages because they focus only on their partner's flaws. But if you focus on the 90 percent of your partner's good qualities and overlook the 10 percent that bothers you, thanksgiving will come more easily.

Jesus' Key to Feeding the 5,000

With just five loaves and two fish, Jesus didn't complain. Instead, "He took the five loaves, and the two fishes, and looking up to heaven, he blessed, and brake, and gave the loaves to his disciples, and the disciples to the multitude" (Matthew 14:19). His thanksgiving released a miracle, and the food multiplied to feed thousands. Let's learn to give thanks, even when it's hard, so we can release God's presence and power in our lives.

Colossians 4:3

"Withal praying also for us, that God would open unto us a door of utterance, to speak the mystery of Christ, for which I am also in bonds."

PAUL'S REQUEST FOR PRAYER

Even the great apostle Paul needed prayer. This shows that no matter how anointed or experienced we are, we all need the support of others' prayers.

1. Prayer for Preaching Opportunities

"That God would open unto us a door of utterance"

Throughout his ministry, Paul faced many obstacles. For example, in Philippi, he cast out an evil spirit from a girl, only to be beaten, jailed, and driven out of the city (Acts 16:16-24). The devil often used people to hinder Paul's work.

I've experienced similar hindrances. Sometimes, when I'm invited to speak at a church, unexpected problems arise to block me. When this happens, I know God is about to do something mighty in that place.

My Passport Went Missing

Once I was supposed to fly out to preach, but my passport went missing. The embassy couldn't find it, and I knew it was a trick of the devil to stop me. I prayed, and eventually, they found and released my passport. When I finally arrived at that place to speak, there was a mighty move of God.

The Devil Can Use People, Circumstances, and Even Natural Events to Hinder Us

In the book of Job, the devil used the Sabeans to steal Job's oxen and donkeys and kill his servants (Job 1:14-15). He also used a great wind to destroy the house where Job's children were feasting, killing them all (Job 1:18-19).

Paul understood that the devil could hinder, delay, or block his ministry. That's why he asked for prayer. The same applies to us. Whether it's a business contract, a ministry opportunity, or a personal goal, the devil can use people or circumstances to stand in the way. That's why we must pray for open doors and divine access.

Colossians 4:4

"That I may make it manifest, as I ought to speak."

PAUL'S REQUEST FOR PRAYER continued

2. Prayer to Speak the Mysteries of God

The Word of God is mysterious or difficult to understand for several reasons. Here are a couple of them.

a. *Spiritual Blindness*

"In whom the god of this world hath blinded the minds of them which believe not, lest the light of the glorious gospel of Christ, who is the image of God, should shine unto them" (2 Corinthians 4:4). Sin blinds people spiritually and prevents them from accessing the spirit realm. This makes it difficult for many, especially those who are not born again, to understand the mysteries in God's Word.

b. Revelation

The Holy Spirit has to reveal or uncover the spirit realm before you can understand it. "But even unto this day, when Moses is read, the vail is upon their heart. Nevertheless when it shall turn to the Lord, the vail shall be taken away. Now the Lord is that Spirit: and where the Spirit of the Lord is, there is liberty" (2 Corinthians 3:15-17).

There is a curtain or veil in the spirit realm that has to be removed before you can understand God's Word. The only person who can do that is the Holy Spirit. He is the only One who has the power to change you. You can hear a good sermon and not change, because the Holy Spirit was not involved. He is the only One who has transformational powers. "But we all, with open face beholding as in a glass the glory of the Lord, are changed into the same image from glory to glory, even as by the Spirit of the Lord" (2 Corinthians 3:18).

Colossians 4:5

"Walk in wisdom toward them that are without, redeeming the time."

HOW TO WALK IN WISDOM

1. Walk in Wisdom by Using Time Effectively

"Redeeming the time"

The phrase "redeeming the time" means to rescue time from loss or waste. In other words, use time efficiently. Paul emphasizes that how we use time is a clear indicator of wisdom. This is a practical and timeless principle.

Time Is a Precious Resource

Time is a universal resource—everyone, whether rich or poor, young or old, has 24 hours in a day. The difference lies in how we use time. Paul challenges us to see time as a valuable resource and use it wisely.

For example, if you're a student, your success depends on how efficiently you use your time. Instead of spending hours watching movies or scrolling through social media, dedicate time to studying, praying, and personal development. "The race is not to the swift, nor the battle to the strong, neither yet bread to the wise, nor yet riches to men of understanding, nor yet favour to men of skill; but time and chance happeneth to them all" (Ecclesiastes 9:11). This means success isn't just about talent or strength but about how we use the time and opportunities presented to us.

Use the Advantage of Time

An investment of $1,000 a year at a compound interest of 10 percent will yield $164,490 in thirty years. That's the power of time. This gives you an average of $2.74 savings a day. I believe many people can afford that.

Similarly, in our spiritual lives, waking up early to pray and spend time with God is an efficient use of time. Jesus Himself demonstrated this: "And in the morning, rising up a great while before day, He went out, and departed into a solitary place, and there prayed" (Mark 1:35).

Colossians 4:6

"Let your speech be always with grace, seasoned with salt, that ye may know how ye ought to answer every man."

HOW TO SPEAK

1. Speak with Grace

"Let your speech be always with grace"

One of the definitions of grace is "divine influence." This means the Holy Spirit should influence the words we speak. Sometimes you feel a gentle prick on your heart when you are about to say something you should not say. That's the Holy Spirit ministering grace.

2. Speak Words of Peace

"Seasoned with salt"

What does this mean? This Scripture offers a clue. "Salt is good: but if the salt have lost his saltness, wherewith will ye season it? Have salt in yourselves, and have peace one with another" (Mark 9:50).

Here salt is symbolic of peace. Our words will foster peace when it's seasoned with salt. In a marital misunderstanding, our words must eventually foster peace instead of insults and abuse. Some people have acidic tongues; their words create conflict and destroy relationships. This is not a mark of wisdom. "If it be possible, as much as lieth in you, live peaceably with all men" (Romans 12:18).

3. Use the Appropriate Words

"You may know how you ought to answer every man"

It takes self-control and wisdom to give the right responses, especially in a heated and tense atmosphere. Only the Holy Spirit can give you the power to do that. Words can break your children and cost you your job.

In a marriage, replacing insults with words of love and affirmation can strengthen the relationship. The same applies to parenting, friendships, and all other interactions. When our words are filled with grace, they build up rather than tear down.

Colossians 4:7

"All my state shall Tychicus declare unto you, who is a beloved brother, and a faithful minister and fellowservant in the Lord."

THE IMPORTANCE OF RELATIONSHIPS

The end of Colossians chapter 4 is filled with greetings. At first glance, these greetings might seem like simple, insignificant words. However, "All scripture is given by inspiration of God, and is profitable" (2 Timothy 3:16). Even these greetings hold valuable lessons for us.

Every relationship has a unique purpose. If we can identify the purpose of a relationship, we can maximize its benefits. But if we don't, we risk missing out on what God intends for us through that relationship.

The Example of Laban and Jacob
Laban told Jacob, "I have learned by experience that the LORD hath blessed me for thy sake" (Genesis 30:27). Laban recognized that Jacob was a source of blessing in his life. Similarly, some people in your life are meant to be sources of blessing, counsel, or encouragement. As we examine Paul's relationships, think about your own relationships and discern their purposes. This will help you avoid frustration and make the most of every connection.

1. "Tychicus"

Tychicus played a significant role in Paul's ministry. He was the one who delivered Paul's letter to the Colossians. That was a very important assignment. Imagine what we would have lost if he had misplaced it.

THE PURPOSE OF TYCHICUS' VISIT

1. To Bring a Report About Him

"All my state shall Tychicus declare unto you"
Tychicus was to update the church on how Paul was faring. Remember, Paul was in prison, and the church was concerned about his well-being. When was the last time you checked on your pastor, boss, or spiritual leader? Often people forget that leaders are human too and need encouragement.

WHO WAS TYCHICUS TO PAUL?

1. He Was a Close Friend

"A beloved brother"
The term "brother" signifies a deep, familial bond. "Let brotherly love continue" (Hebrews 13:1). This reminds us that everyone needs close friends.

Some people pride themselves on having no friends, saying, "I don't need anyone; I'm fine alone." But this isn't something to boast about. God created us as social beings. In Genesis 2:18, He said, "It is not good that the man should be alone" (Genesis 2:18). We need close friends; people we can share our hearts, fears, and dreams with without fear of judgment or betrayal.

2. He Was a Servant

"A faithful minister"

The Greek word for minister here is *diakonos*, which means someone who serves or runs errands. Tychicus wasn't a preacher or evangelist; his role was practical. He helped advance God's work behind the scenes.

This is a powerful reminder that not everyone is called to preach or lead worship. Some serve by running errands, managing logistics, or supporting others. In Acts 6:1-4, the apostles appointed deacons to handle practical tasks so they could focus on prayer and preaching. Both roles are essential to God's work.

I Work with Many Helpers in My Ministry

For example, in my ministry, I work with many wonderful people behind the scenes: Priscilla, Benji, Ebo, etc. When I preach, a team of technical staff works behind the scenes. Some operate cameras, type notes, and manage various social media platforms. They may not be visible, but their work is vital. God remembers and rewards every act of service, whether seen or unseen.

The Importance of Physical Service

In the Old Testament, the Levites were divided into groups. Only a few, like the priests, interacted directly with God in the tabernacle. Others, like the Gershonites, were responsible for carrying and maintaining the tabernacle's materials (Numbers 4:24-28). Both groups were serving God, even though their tasks differed.

Similarly, in the church today, some focus on the spiritual aspects of ministry, while others handle practical tasks. Both are equally important. "For as the body is one, and hath many members, and all the members of that one body, being many, are one body: so also is Christ" (1 Corinthians 12:12).

If you're serving in a physical way, whether it's cleaning the church, managing finances, or running errands, don't think your work is less significant. God sees and values your contribution. The key is to do everything "heartily, as to the Lord, and not unto men" (Colossians 3:23).

3. He Was a Co-slave

"Fellowservant"

The word "servant" in Greek is *doulos*, which means a slave. In those days, slaves had no will of their own. They couldn't choose where to sleep, what to do, or even what time to work. Tychicus was a slave of God. This meant Tychicus had surrendered his will entirely to God, allowing the Lord to make all his decisions.

The Example of Jesus

Jesus prayed, "Father, if thou be willing, remove this cup from me: nevertheless not my will, but thine, be done" (Luke 22:42). Immediately after this surrender, an angel appeared to strengthen Him (Luke 22:43). When we surrender our will to God, we release the ministry of angels in our lives. You don't even have to ask for angelic help. Simply yielding to God's will invites His supernatural assistance.

Colossians 4:8

"Whom I have sent unto you for the same purpose, that he might know your estate, and comfort your hearts."

THE PURPOSE OF TYCHICUS' VISIT continued

2. To Bring a Report (Estate) About Them

"That he might know your estate"

Tychicus was supposed to bring a report about the Colossian church back to Paul. This shows the importance of staying connected and sharing updates within the body of Christ.

3. To Comfort Them

"Comfort your hearts"
He was also a source of comfort. Some people have a unique ability to bring peace and reassurance. When you're around them, your burdens feel lighter. Paul needed such people in his life, and so do we.

How God Comforted Paul through Titus
"For, when we were come into Macedonia, our flesh had no rest, but we were troubled on every side; without were fightings, within were fears. Nevertheless, God, that comforteth those that are cast down, comforted us by the coming of Titus" (2 Corinthians 7:5-6). This reminds us that while the Holy Spirit is our ultimate Comforter, God also uses people to bring us comfort.

The Old Man with No Help
I once saw an old man in the UK struggling to push his shopping cart. He could barely walk, yet there was no one to help him. The Holy Spirit spoke to me and said, "This man lived only for himself. He never helped anyone, and now he has no one to comfort him." This was a sobering reminder that we reap what we sow.

If we invest in others, we'll have people to comfort us in our time of need. "Be not deceived; God is not mocked: for whatsoever a man soweth, that shall he also reap" (Galatians 6:7). Let's take time to invest in people—helping, encouraging, and comforting them. One day we'll need the same support, and God will send someone to comfort us.

Colossians 4:9

"With Onesimus, a faithful and beloved brother, who is one of you. They shall make known unto you all things which are done here."

THE IMPORTANCE OF RELATIONSHIPS continued

2. Onesimus
This is how Paul described him.

a. Faithful

It is not easy to find faithful friends, employees, and even spouses. But God blessed Paul with a faithful man. "Most men will proclaim every one his own goodness: but a faithful man who can find?" (Proverbs 20:6). Pray that the Lord will bless you with faithful people.

b. Beloved Brother

Paul called him a brother. There are friends who end up being like brothers. "A man that hath friends must shew himself friendly: and there is a friend that sticketh closer than a brother" (Proverbs 18:24).

c. His assignment

To tell them of what was being done by Paul and the others with him.

Colossians 4:10

Aristarchus my fellow prisoner saluteth you, and Marcus, sister's son to Barnabas, (touching whom ye received commandments: if he come unto you, receive him)."

THE IMPORTANCE OF RELATIONSHIPS continued

3. Aristarchus

a. Paul's Fellow Prisoner Salutes Them

There are people we empathize with because we are in the same situation.

b. Marcus' Sister's Son

He sent greetings to Barnabas.

4. Barnabas

He visited them earlier with some commands and will be coming again. He admonishes them to receive him when he comes.

Colossians 4:11

"And Jesus, which is called Justus, who are of the circumcision. These only are my fellowworkers unto the kingdom of God, which have been a comfort unto me."

THE IMPORTANCE OF RELATIONSHIPS continued

5. Jesus Called Justus

"And Jesus, which is called Justus, who are of the circumcision"

Paul describes Jesus (Justus) as being "of the circumcision," meaning he was a converted Jew. God established circumcision as a sign of His covenant with Abraham and his descendants (Genesis 17:11). For Jews, circumcision was a physical marker of their identity.

By mentioning this, Paul highlights that Justus was a Jew who had become a follower of Jesus. This was significant because in those days converting to Christianity could be dangerous for Jews. Justus's faith was a bold and costly decision.

Today a converted Muslim came to see me. I was encouraged by his faith because I knew what he had been through with his Muslim family because of this. Our lives can be an encouragement to people when we live for the Lord.

   a.   *He Was a Fellow Worker*

"Fellow worker"

Paul calls Justus a "fellow worker." This indicates that their relationship was also based on shared ministry and mission. Unlike Tychicus, who was a close friend, Justus was more of a colleague. Their bond was rooted in their work for the Kingdom of God.

This teaches us about situational relationships. Some people are in our lives because of shared assignments or goals. These relationships are important, but they may not be as deep or enduring as others. Recognizing this helps us manage expectations and avoid unnecessary frustration.

For example, if you work with someone in a church or office, your relationship may be tied to that context. When the assignment ends, the relationship might change, and that's okay.

Understanding this dynamic helps us appreciate each relationship for what it is.

A Word to Pastors and Members

Paul mentions Justus as one of his few fellow workers. There is always a shortage of laborers in the Kingdom. It was said of Jesus, "But when he saw the multitudes, he was moved with compassion on them, because they fainted, and were scattered abroad, as sheep having no shepherd. Then saith he unto his disciples, The harvest truly is plenteous, but the labourers are few" (Matthew 9:36-37).

This is a reminder to pastors and church leaders that finding committed workers is always a challenge. Even in Paul's time, there were only a few who stood with him. If you're a pastor, don't be discouraged by the shortage of laborers. Focus on those who are willing and faithful, and pray and trust God to send more workers.

For church members, this is a call to step up and serve. The church isn't a spectator sport; it's a body where every member has a role to play. Whether your role is big or small, what matters is that you're fulfilling the function God has given you.

b. He Comforted Paul

"Which have been a comfort unto me"

Paul's relationship with Justus also teaches us about the importance of comfort in our lives. While the Holy Spirit is our ultimate Comforter, God often uses people to bring us comfort. Paul writes, "If there be therefore any consolation in Christ, if any comfort of love, if any fellowship of the Spirit, if any bowels and mercies, Fulfil ye my joy, that ye be likeminded, having the same love, being of one accord, of one mind" (Philippians 2:1-2).

If you've been isolating yourself, it's time to reconnect. Don't cut yourself off from the body of Christ. Relationships are a vital part of God's design for our lives.

> *Colossians 4:12*
>
> *"Epaphras, who is one of you, a servant of Christ, saluteth you, always labouring fervently for you in prayers, that ye may stand perfect and complete in all the will of God."*

THE IMPORTANCE OF RELATIONSHIPS continued

6. Epaphras

a. He Was a Native of Colossae

"Epaphras, who is one of you"

There are certain people that only you can reach. Why? Because you're one of them. There are some people in the clubs that only club girls can reach because you used to be one of them. If a pastor goes, they won't listen. So Paul said Epaphras is of Colossae. He came to Colossae and established a church. You should listen to him because he's one of you.

I just want you to know that there is somebody that only you can reach because you're one of them. Sometimes you are the only one who can reach out to the boys you used to hang out with every Friday. You are the only person the prostitutes will listen to. Why? Because you used to be one of them, they can identify with you more than a doctor.

Maybe you come from a certain country or a certain tribe, or you speak a certain language. You are the only person who can reach them. People find it easier to receive from people who are just like them.

So I want to encourage you. There is somebody waiting for you, somebody in your inner circle, somebody who is just like you. He doesn't like talking. He's just like you. When you talk to him, he will understand. I want you to make it a point to reach out to that person because you are a member of God's body.

b. Epaphras Greeted Them

"Saluteth you"

He greeted or saluted them. He said, "I want you to greet everyone for me." That's powerful.

c. He Had Been Praying for Them

"Always labouring fervently for you in prayers"
Epaphras had a specialised function. There are relationships that are specialised. The job of this man was to pray.

My Job Is to Pray for My Church Members and Others
I'm a pastor, and most of the time, do you know what I'm doing? I'm praying for my church members. I'm praying for so many things. I may not visit them at home, but I'm praying for them. That's my job.

As a prophet. I'm always interceding and praying for people. Once people understand your function, they will appreciate you more. Jesus said to Simon Peter, "Satan has desired to have you, that he may shift you as wheat." But then He said, "I have prayed for thee" (Luke 22:31-32). He said, "I'll be in the background praying for you."

That's why it's important to be part of a church. There are people in a church whose job is to pray for you; for example, prayer warriors. They're praying for you, and you must appreciate them. You must also make your contribution to the body of Christ, because in Christianity, we are not supposed to have a parasitic relationship. It's a symbiotic relationship. We are all contributing.

TWO PRAYERS OF EPAPHRAS

a. For Them to Be Matured

"That ye may stand perfect"
That's a prayer topic straight from the Holy Ghost. You can also pray for maturity. That God will help you to grow spiritually.

b. For Them to Walk Completely in the Will of God

"Complete in all the will of God"
The word "complete" means to fulfill God's will in every area of our lives: work, marriage, church, etc. The will of God is revealed in the Scriptures and by the Holy Spirit.

Focusing on Jesus Helps to Complete Your Assignment

"Looking unto Jesus the author and finisher of our faith; who for the joy that was set before him endured the cross, despising the shame, and is set down at the right hand of the throne of God" (Hebrews 12:2). If you don't focus on Jesus, you cannot walk completely in God's will. If you're married and don't focus on Jesus, bitterness can destroy the marriage. If you're in church and don't focus on Jesus, maybe somebody will say something you don't like—and it'll cause you to leave.

In relationships, it's essential to focus on Jesus because human beings will hurt you—but remember, you've also hurt somebody. Before you take the speck out of your brother's eye, remove the beam from your own (Matthew 7:5).

People who don't look at Jesus struggle with stable relationships. They react to their hurts and pain. But we must look to Jesus, knowing He called us, He saved us, and He will complete His work in us. When He's your source, your sustenance, your supply, and your blessing, you'll always have joy and fulfill your assignment.

Colossians 4:13

"For I bear him record, that he hath a great zeal for you, and them that are in Laodicea, and them in Hierapolis."

TESTIMONY ABOUT EPAPHRAS

c. *He Was Zealous*

"He hath a great zeal"

Not everyone is zealous, but it's powerful when you meet believers burning with fire. Tell them, "Church starts at 8 a.m.," and they arrive at 6 a.m. These are the zealous ones!

Epaphras wasn't just concerned about himself or his family; he cared for souls in multiple cities: Colosse, Laodicea, and Hierapolis. Zeal is required to work for God.

Paul Himself Was a Man of Zeal

He wrote: "Of the Jews five times received I forty stripes save one. Thrice was I beaten with rods, once was I stoned, thrice I suffered shipwreck, a night and a day I have been in the deep" (2 Corinthians 11:24–25). Paul endured everything for the Gospel. So if he called Epaphras zealous, that man must have been extraordinary!

I want to encourage you to be a zealous Christian. Dull faith won't reach anyone. Without zeal, you can't win souls, minister, or preach effectively.

Prayer and the Word of God Generate Zeal

On the day of Pentecost, "there appeared unto them cloven tongues like as of fire, and it sat upon each of them" (Acts 2:3). This fire was a result of them spending time in prayer.

Jeremiah also speaks of this fire through reading the Word of God. "His word was in mine heart as a burning fire shut up in my bones, and I was weary with forbearing, and I could not stay" (Jeremiah 20:9).

If you feel like your fire has gone down, return to prayer and the Word. Spend time in God's presence, meditate on His Word, and let His Spirit reignite the fire within you.

Colossians 4:14

"Luke, the beloved physician, and Demas, greet you."

THE IMPORTANCE OF RELATIONSHIPS continued

7. Luke

"Luke, the beloved physician"

Luke was a doctor and the author of the Gospel of Luke and the book of Acts. He was the only Gentile to write a Gospel, and his writings provide a detailed account of Jesus' life and the early church.

Luke was a faithful companion to Paul, traveling with him and assisting him in his ministry. Though he was often in the background, his contributions were invaluable. He didn't seek the spotlight but served quietly and faithfully.

This teaches us the importance of being a supportive presence in the lives of others. Not everyone is called to be in the forefront, but everyone has a role to play. Whether you're assisting a leader, serving behind the scenes, or documenting God's Word, your contribution matters.

8. Demas

"Demas, greets you"
Paul also mentions Demas, but unlike Luke, he doesn't say much about him. He simply states, "Demas greeteth you." This lack of commentary is disturbing.

Demas Forsakes Paul
Later, Paul reveals that "Demas hath forsaken me, having loved this present world" (2 Timothy 4:10).

Demas started well but fell away because he loved the world more than God. His story serves as a warning to all of us. It's possible to begin with zeal and passion but lose our way if we're not careful. We must guard our hearts and stay rooted in our relationship with God.

If you know someone who is drifting away from God, pray for them. And if you feel yourself growing cold spiritually, return to God. His arms are always open to receive you.

Colossians 4:15-16

"Salute the brethren which are in Laodicea, and Nymphas, and the church which is in his house. And when this epistle is read among you, cause that it be read also in the church of the Laodiceans; and that ye likewise read the epistle from Laodicea."

THE IMPORTANCE OF RELATIONSHIPS continued

PAUL GREETS THEM

"Salute the brethren"
Paul saluted the Christians in Laodicea and Nymphas and the church that was in his house.

A church wasn't defined by a building, a pulpit, or a choir. It was simply a gathering of believers.

Two or Three People Make a Church
Jesus said, "For where two or three are gathered together in my name, there am I in the midst of them" (Matthew 18:20). This means you can have a church in your home. You don't need elaborate setups or programs. All you need is a few believers coming together to pray, study the Word, and encourage one another.

This is a call to return to the simplicity of the Gospel. Start a Bible study group in your home. Gather your family or friends for prayer. You don't need a name, a banner, or a constitution. Just gather in Jesus' name, and He will be there.

Colossians 4:17

"Say to Archippus, Take heed to the ministry which thou hast received in the Lord, that thou fulfil it."

THE IMPORTANCE OF RELATIONSHIPS continued

9. Archippus

Paul Warned Him to Focus on His Ministry
It's easy to get distracted by what others are doing or to desire ministries that seem more glamorous. But God has given each of us a unique assignment, and we must focus on that.

How Satan Fell
Satan's downfall began when he said, "I will ascend into heaven, I will exalt my throne above the stars of God...I will be like the most High" (Isaiah 14:13-14). He wanted what wasn't his. In contrast, Jesus said, "Not my will, but thine, be done" (Luke 22:42).

We must ask God, "What will You have me to do?" (Acts 9:6). Don't chase after positions or titles. Focus on the ministry God has given you.

Archippus was to carry out his ministry with dedication and commitment. Every ministry requires sacrifice, hard work, and perseverance. Whether you're called to preach, teach, pray, or serve in any way, you must be willing to put in the effort.

Success in ministry isn't about popularity or recognition. It's about faithfulness to God's calling. Paul told Timothy, "Do the work of an evangelist, make full proof of thy ministry" (2 Timothy 4:5).

Colossians 4:18

"The salutation by the hand of me Paul. Remember my bonds. Grace be with you. Amen."

FINAL WORDS FROM PAUL

"The salutation by the hand of me Paul"
Paul personally signs off the letter, emphasizing its authenticity and his personal connection to the Colossians. This reminds us of the importance of personal touch in our relationships. Whether it's a handwritten note, a phone call, or a simple greeting, taking the time to connect personally can make a big difference.

PAUL REMINDED THEM THAT HE WAS IN PRISON

"Remember my bonds"
This wasn't just a request for sympathy; it was a call to action. The Colossian church responded by sending Epaphras to care for Paul.

This teaches us to remember those who are suffering, especially for the sake of the Gospel. Whether it's a missionary, a pastor, or a fellow believer going through a tough time, we can support them through prayer, encouragement, and practical help.

PAUL ENDS WITH A PRAYER FOR GRACE

"Grace be with you"
Grace is God's unmerited favor and empowerment to do what we cannot do on our own. "For by grace are ye saved through faith; and that not of yourselves: it is the gift of God: Not of works, lest any man should boast" (Ephesians 2:8-9).

Grace is essential for every area of our lives—spiritual growth, relationships, ministry, and even daily tasks. Without grace, we cannot reach our full potential or fulfill God's purpose for our lives.

Paul often began his letters with prayers for grace, mercy, and peace. These three elements are foundational for a thriving Christian life.

CONCLUSION

I trust you have been blessed by this study. As you apply the things learned, I want to pray that you will experience the grace of God and promotion in your life.

Father, in Jesus' name, Your Word says that You lift the poor from the dust and the needy from the ash heap, seating them with princes (Psalm 113:7-8). I pray for Your grace to abound in the lives of everyone reading this book. Some have been stuck for too long: spiritually, financially, maritally, or in their plans and dreams.

I pray for a divine shift. Let the wind of the Holy Spirit blow in their lives, just as it blew on the day of Pentecost and transformed a small group of believers into a mighty church (Acts 2:1-4).

I break every curse, every demonic stronghold, and every human barrier holding them back. I rebuke every force that has anchored them to the ground and prevented them from moving forward. I declare promotion over their lives: spiritual promotion, financial promotion, marital promotion, and promotion in every area where they've been stuck. Let the wind of the Spirit blow, and may they rise to new levels of faith, favor, and fruitfulness. In Jesus' mighty name. Amen.

ABOUT THE AUTHOR

Kakra Baiden is a Christian pastor, revivalist, author, teacher, and conference speaker known for his prophetic gifts and miracle anointing. He is known as "The Walking Bible" for his supernatural ability to teach and preach the Word of God from memory.

Pastor Baiden is an architect by profession and currently serves as the resident bishop of the Elaia City Church, Accra, Ghana.

He is also the founder of Airpower Ministry, a ministry through which he touches the world through books, videos, social media, and international conferences. His daily radio and TV program, *Airpower with Kakra Baiden*, reaches millions daily, in over 60 countries in different languages with signs and wonders. This program also airs on *TBN Africa*. In Ghana, his programs can be heard in different local dialects on over 60 radio stations and on the major television network, TV3, which covers the whole country. He has ministered the Word on every continent and is also the author of the best-selling book, *Squatters*, and others.

Pastor Baiden is married to Lady Rev. Dr. Ewuradwoa Baiden and they have four children.

www.ingramcontent.com/pod-product-compliance
Lightning Source LLC
Chambersburg PA
CBHW070456100426
42743CB00010B/1651